Billy,

After you read this book there is only one rule: Don't bore Mum with the details.

Love
Sean

THE DREAM RYDER CUP

THE DREAM RYDER CUP

DEREK LAWRENSON

BLANDFORD

*For my mother and father, who gave so that I might receive,
and my wife Paula, for making it all worthwhile.*

A BLANDFORD BOOK

First published in the UK by Blandford
An imprint of the Cassell Group
Cassell plc, Wellington House,
125 Strand, London WC2R 0BB

Photographs supplied by Phil Sheldon Picture Library

Distributed in the United States by Sterling Publishing Co., Inc.,
387 Park Avenue South, New York, NY 10016–8810

Distributed in Australia by Capricorn Link (Australia) Pty Ltd
2/13 Carrington Road, Castle Hill, NSW 2154

British Library Cataloguing-in-Publication Data
A catalogue entry for this title is available from the British Library

ISBN 0–7137–2525–7

Typeset by
Cambrian Typesetters, Frimley, Surrey
Printed and bound in Great Britain by
Hartnolls Ltd, Bodmin

Contents

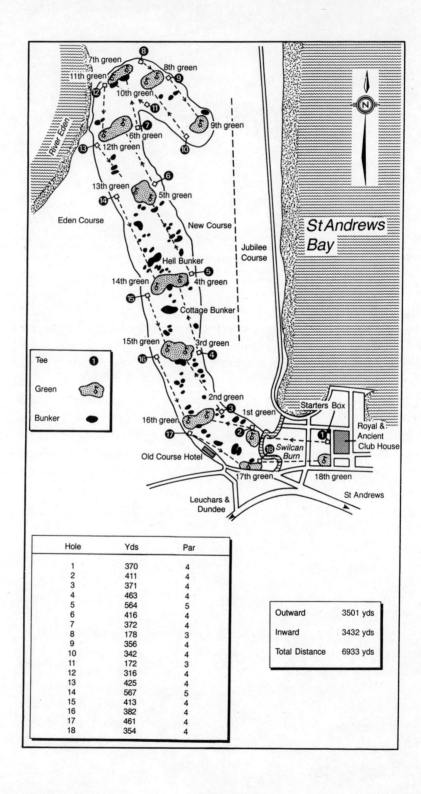

Hole	Yds	Par
1	370	4
2	411	4
3	371	4
4	463	4
5	564	5
6	416	4
7	372	4
8	178	3
9	356	4
10	342	4
11	172	3
12	316	4
13	425	4
14	567	5
15	413	4
16	382	4
17	461	4
18	354	4

Outward	3501 yds
Inward	3432 yds
Total Distance	6933 yds

Introduction

WHEN I WAS growing up in Liverpool a game my father and I had endless enjoyment playing was deciding who were the best eleven players to have represented the football club that was such an important part of both our lives.

As the team was dominating Europe at the time and winning the League Championship and the FA Cup almost as a matter of routine, it was tempting just to copy that week's team sheet. But a place had to be found for Billy Liddell, of course. And how could you leave Sir Roger Hunt out? And then there were Ian St John and big Ron Yeats. We were off. The game would last for hours. The worst part was trying to find a place for Tommy Smith. 'I've got to go with Alan Hansen and Mark Lawrenson,' I'd say, and then I'd be overcome with guilt. You see, I'd witnessed Smithy on a number of occasions hobbling along to the match on knees that had given out after all the years of strain. I'd asked him once whether it was all worth it and he'd replied: 'Son, you're a Liverpool supporter. What do you think?'

How on earth could I even contemplate leaving out a player who so loved turning out for his team that he thought it easily worth the sacrifice of not being able to walk properly in later life?

Of course, as I got older I realized that everyone was playing this game of choosing dream teams. Now it's a national pastime. There's hardly a sport on either side of the Atlantic where a fantasy league doesn't exist.

Sport is nothing if not the fulfilment of dreams, is it? Who hasn't watched Severiano Ballesteros in action without thinking that this is the realization of the game as one hoped it would be played?

David Gower's languid drives, Michael Jordan's prodigious leaps, Ryan Giggs's silken touchline runs, Joe Montana's laser-beamed passes: what are these thrilling things if not examples of sport that is heaven-sent?

When Rod Dymott, the publisher of Blandford, approached me with the idea for this book I was immediately intrigued. A dream match between the best-ever Ryder Cup players from America and those from Europe? All the possibilities raced through my mind. Who would I choose? How would it work?

Clearly, there were some ground rules that I would have to impose on myself. They would all have to play with the same equipment, for a start.

I've set the book in the modern era although no precise date is envisaged. I've handicapped both teams by choosing Walter Hagen and Tony Jacklin as non-playing captains. Certainly both would normally walk into their respective sides. But having set the book in this day and age I didn't feel the idea of having *playing* captains was realistic. I chose those two because in a playing sense I felt they were roughly similar in terms of their value to their teams and so the loss was equal; and time has recognized them as perhaps the most noted captains that the contest has seen.

Selecting the two teams gave me difficulty only in the last few names for each side. I felt that Ballesteros, Cotton, Faldo, Langer, Olazabal, Woosnam, Lyle and O'Connor just couldn't be left out of any European team. Similarly Sarazen, Palmer, Nicklaus, Watson, Nelson (Byron, not Larry), Snead, Trevino, Hogan and Casper had to play for America.

Four left to find for Europe then: four hundred or so to choose from. I went for Barnes and Gallacher because they were such a good foursomes and fourballs pairing. I plumped for Oosterhuis for his partnership with Faldo. I went for Eric Brown because of his indomitable spirit, his record of invincibility in singles and the fact that he would be interesting to write about.

For the Americans, Mangrum was given the nod because of his partnership with Snead; Lema because he won the Open at St Andrews and would surely have gone on to become one of the great players but for his tragic death in a plane crash; and Kite because he has proven himself time and again in the Ryder Cup.

All right, I can hear you say: how can you leave out Dai Rees? Where are Colin Montgomerie, Percy and Peter Alliss, and Harry

Weetman? Surely Open champions like Max Faulkner and Fred Daly were worth places?

Once you get into the book it will become clear that leaving out Rees, in particular, caused me a lot of angst.

If at the end you still think I got it wrong, think of it this way: am I the first person to have selected a Ryder Cup team with whom you've disagreed? Exactly.

As for the Americans, Demaret's record of six wins out of six, and the fact that some of his best years were lost to the war, made him difficult to omit; Azinger, Littler, Irwin and Larry Nelson all had cases; and in particular I agonized over leaving out Johnny Miller and Raymond Floyd. Even now I'm not sure I got it right.

Although all the players were selected for what they achieved or have achieved to date in their careers, they're not all the same age in the book. It would just not have had the right ring, although I have denied no player any of his triumphs.

Anyway, Nicklaus is in his prime; so is Hogan. Palmer and Sarazen are at the veteran stage, as is Cotton. Watson is a few years younger than now. Most of the current players are their present ages.

The venue? There could be only one. It may never have hosted a Ryder Cup match and indeed it has a lot stacked against it in these days of mass crowds and mass commercialism. But for a dream match it has to be St Andrews.

It is an obvious point but worth stating: this is a work of fiction – not only the match itself but some aspects of the personalities of the main characters. We are all shaped by the circumstances in which we find ourselves and so when drawing in the likes of Nelson and Cotton I felt I had to take into account that the world in which I've placed them is drastically different from the one in which they played the game. Similarly I doubt very much whether Hagen would be quite so keen these days to turn up for play still wearing his tuxedo from the night before (this was actually a ruse on many occasions during his prime to make people think he was more of a party animal than was the case). Imagine what coverage that would now make in the newspapers! I thought about drawing upon such antics but over a book's length, I felt, the fantasy has to convey a sense of reality to sustain it. Still, I've not changed him too much, nor the other main players. The more you read about golf the more you come to love Hagen in particular. He was the sport's Muhammad Ali. Having covered the professional golf circuit for the past twelve years, including six Ryder Cups, I have obviously found writing about today's players less of a problem. But equally I've now put them with people they've never met in their lives. How would they react? I hope no one is offended by my feverish imagination.

Being a novel of sorts the book has been written in the past tense throughout. I thought about adopting the present tense for character points, such as 'Hagen practises assiduously', or 'Palmer is at an age that . . .'. In the end I decided that these players are so fixed in the reader's mind in a certain time frame that it sounded both incongruous, and also, in the case of those who are no longer with us, a little tasteless. Finally, I've no desire to shatter illusions unduly and so the dialogue in this book is virtually free of four-letter words. It may lose something in authenticity but I just felt that such language would have gone against the grain of what this was supposed to be all about.

I hope you enjoy the book in the spirit in which it was written. It is meant not as a work of record but as a work of love, based on one writer's personal experience of the golf world and its characters, and the premise that sport weaves its magic best when we're living in a dream world.

Oh, and by the way: Clemence; Neal, Hansen, Lawrenson (no relation, alas), Byrne; Keegan, Souness, Barnes, Liddell; Dalglish, Rush. (Many apologies, Smithy. And you too, Sir Roger.)

Derek Lawrenson

1

Monday: Arrival

THIS IS THE story of a unique Ryder Cup; unique in the sense that the writer, myself, was given unprecedented access to all the players and their innermost thoughts.

Maybe it was because I was so close to these people that I have come to look upon it as the greatest of all Ryder Cups, but many others have said these words without having had the benefit of my vantage point. Perhaps you feel the same about it yourself. Certainly, everything felt right that week. The Old Course had never looked better. Many of the players have never performed better. The two captains were courageous and inspirational. The weather was a perfect mix of the sublime and the ridiculous. The crowds were huge and partisan but sportsmanlike. The town was a riot of colour and laughter. The university filled its days with learning and its evenings with stories of what had unfolded down the road. The bars exaggerated the admittedly great actions that the patrons had witnessed. The restaurants were the scene for a more sober but still compulsive reflection of affairs. Only the cinema and the St Andrews theatre stood empty, as if people couldn't bear to be silent and therefore unable to talk about this, perhaps as great a sporting event as this country has witnessed. And all the while the sea flowed into St Andrews Bay and then ebbed, taking with it the deeds of legend.

What this story sets out to do is to offer the big picture rather than merely the minutiae of what went on over the Old Course. I have set out to tell a remarkable tale, one that reveals the intrigue and the planning and the sheer bravado that go with the Ryder

Cup. I count myself incredibly fortunate to have been given so much hitherto classified information.

Here it is then, the most comprehensive reading yet of a Ryder Cup that thoroughly lived up to all of the eager anticipation. Of seven amazing days in the lives of twenty-six extraordinary sportsmen. Indeed, there were times when I was revising this work that I found I had to pinch my skin to convince myself I had not imagined it all.

Five miles north of St Andrews on a tight and winding road lies the small village of Leuchars, with its magnificent parish church dating back to the late twelfth century. Many believe it to be the finest Norman church in Scotland, and several people were to be found, wrapped up against the chill, wandering in the ornate graveyard inspecting the sixteenth-century tombstones. A far larger crowd had gathered at the RAF base on the outskirts of town. The RAF had moved there in 1920 and now two squadrons, Trouble One and Forty-three, were often to be heard practising manoeuvres in their Tornado Three jets. Today the jets were silent. It was a maintenance day, for one thing. But the faces pressed against the perimeter fencing and the cars that completely encircled the airfield suggested that something altogether more novel was happening than the oft-heard sound of jets roaring away over the North Sea to intercept imaginary bombers.

At 4 p.m., Concorde was due to land, laden with the greatest assembly of golfing talent that any one plane had ever transported across the Atlantic. While the European side had been gathering in dribs and drabs all day at the Old Course Hotel at St Andrews, the American captain, Walter Hagen, had insisted that his players travel as a team. In truth, the plane had landed at Leuchars twice in previous years, bringing players who were due to play in the Open Championship. But this was the Ryder Cup, and the first time it had been staged at the Home of Golf at that. The locals were keen to get an early glimpse of what their team would be up against. The *Dundee Courier* would estimate the crowd to be in the region of 10,000, and as 4 p.m. came and went the first signs of impatience could be seen on the faces of those who had been there for several hours already. Five p.m. came as well without the deafening noise that always precedes Concorde's appearance. If it didn't come soon, then darkness would cloak its arrival, and the hours spent gazing upwards and listening for a tell-tale sound would be largely in vain. What could have kept them?

Actually, what had kept them was a late departure from Washington. Concorde had been due to leave at 7 a.m. but there was absolutely no way that Hagen was ever going to get out of his bed in time to make that appointment. This was truly the morning after the night before. What a time they had enjoyed! If Hagen had been perfectly honest, he would have admitted that dinner with the President and the First Lady was not the way he would have wanted to have spent his final night, prior to the match, on American soil. But Mr President had turned out to be Mr Cool. He even called for his saxophone as the hours turned early and he insisted that Hagen dance with the First Lady. And what a mover she had turned out to be! Hagen had thought her change of appearance from plain university boffin to sophisticated socialite merely one she was obliged to make in accepting her change of territory. But dancing with the American Ryder Cup captain was clearly no chore for her. She was ready to move, and so, of course, was Hagen, the ultimate golfing bon vivant. With Scotch and water in one hand, and partner in the other, he had danced and flirted openly, though not offensively. 'You're my kind of woman,' Hagen said, brazenly, laughing wildly. 'This is my kind of evening,' the First Lady said.

But now it was the following morning and she was up and dressed and studying health care documents. Hagen was far too old to burn the candle at both ends. The team had stayed at the White House but Hagen had not got to bed until 4.30 a.m. The plan had been for the team to gather on the lawns of the White House at 6 a.m. for a group photograph and then they would be taken to the airport in a cavalcade of cars. And, indeed, all the team, bar the captain, were there at 6 a.m. True, the bags under the eyes of Tony Lema and Tom Watson fully indicated that they too had enjoyed their evening – but at least they were there. Hagen was not.

Ben Hogan was furious. The evening wasn't his idea of fun at all. For a start he didn't share the President's view of life, and when The Eagles started playing he realized he didn't share his taste in music either. He said to Byron Nelson: 'There's only one type of eagles that I'm interested in and that's 2 under par.' The plain truth was that he didn't understand his captain. To him, golf was a serious game. It involved complete dedication. What really drove Hogan mad was that people often mixed them up. It had happened at hotels all the time. He would say his name was Hogan and the receptionist would invariably give him messages for Hagen. There was Hogan, expecting messages that in some way related to golf and here he was, being asked to 'come up and see me sometime'. How could two people with names so alike be so different? Even worse: how could the PGA of America make Hagen their Ryder Cup captain? And now he was late for the photoshoot. 'Serves them right,' he thought. He said to Jack Nicklaus: 'How can someone who makes their living in this game, where punctuality is everything, be late for something like this?' 'Relax, Ben,' Nicklaus had said, 'you know Walter always does things slowly.' Nicklaus told him the story that Bobby Jones had related to him, of when Hagen and the great man had played their only head-to-head encounter. Jones was thoroughly irritated by him as well, though for different reasons. Hagen had won the thirty-six-hole match 11 and 10. Jones, whom no one ever accused of sour grapes, said: 'A man who hits the ball down the middle, who puts his second shot on the green, and then 2-putts for par – now I can relate to that. But Walter, he misses his drive, mishits his second shot, and then holes for a birdie; it gets my goat!' If ever a statement summed up how Hagen lived his life then this last one did. He did things in an unorthodox manner but invariably the right result materialized – and with a certain amount of style at that. And now, as the team shuffled their feet on the lawns of the White House, and as the people of St Andrews shuffled their feet at Leuchars, so Hagen appeared, forty-five minutes late, hangover in place, head throbbing. His team knew he was suffering. Everyone could see he was suffering. But Hagen floated down the stairs, on to the lawns, and said: 'What a great day, gentlemen. Let the photo session begin!'

A glass of fruit juice was touching Henry Cotton's lips as Severiano Ballesteros checked in at the Old Course Hotel. The great Spaniard was here with his wife, Carmen, though the children had been left at home in Pedrena. Ballesteros's eldest son, Baldomero, had begged his father to let him come and enjoy the occasion, for, though tender in years, he had already decided to try to follow in his father's footsteps. But the European captain, Tony Jacklin, had been strict on this point: no children. With a child of his own left at home in Florida, Jacklin could not be said to be asking one thing of his players and behaving a different way himself.

Jacklin was talking to Cotton about life on the US Senior tour. All the players were impressed with the way that Jacklin had gone about this new phase in his career, and, more importantly, made it work against all odds. They felt this was a good omen, for the odds were certainly against their winning back the Ryder Cup, which had been lost at The Country Club, in Brookline, Massachusetts, two years earlier. Jacklin had spent the year rushed off his feet. His timetable usually ran something like this: Monday, practise at home in Florida; Tuesday, study the videotapes of the previous week's European tour event, and speak to his vice-captain, Dai Rees, about who was doing what; Wednesday, an early-morning flight to wherever the Senior tour event happened to be, followed by an appearance in the pro-am; Thursday, another pro-am day; Friday to Sunday, the tournament itself; a long flight home on the Sunday evening, and then the whole thing would start again. It was a daunting schedule but in truth he had been delighted when the call came and the Ryder Cup committee had decided that he should be the captain once more. After three Ryder Cups without a victory, it wasn't a total surprise. Jacklin had revitalized European golf before, and now his talismanic presence was required more than ever.

Jacklin left his seat to go over and welcome Ballesteros. The greeting revealed the genuine warmth that each felt for the other. Ballesteros thought that Jacklin should never have left the job as captain. Jacklin thought Ballesteros the greatest natural talent he had seen. And while he accepted that Ballesteros was older now, and the back was occasionally sore, and the nerves not quite as steadfast, he knew how his protégé felt about this match. He knew the depth of Ballesteros's desire to beat the Americans, how it ran to several fathoms ever since that day when the young Spaniard had stepped on to the tee in a US tour event and the announcer, looking down the pairing sheet, had said: 'Now we have, all the way from Spain, Steve Ballesteros.' The American players had teased 'Steve' about this. Hale Irwin had hardly helped matters when, two years later, he called Ballesteros the car park champion after his victory in the Open at Lytham had followed some errant driving and one blow in particular that had finished in a temporary car park. Ballesteros had laughed along, but inside he felt thoroughly insulted. That Spanish pride would forever surface whenever a Ryder Cup was played, and Jacklin knew just how to needle him into producing his best golf.

After the initial greetings had been made Jacklin rejoined Cotton, whose stomach was troubling him. 'Who am I playing with?' 'What time did you say dinner was this evening?' 'What time is the photoshoot in the morning?' 'Why have half the team not checked in yet?' Cotton always had a barrage of questions and Jacklin saw it as his job to calm him down. He didn't want Henry's ulcer playing him up at this stage.

At the bar, Christy O'Connor was enjoying a beer with Ian Woosnam. A couple of people were asking them for autographs but neither player minded the intrusion. Jacklin wanted his players to mingle with the public for most of this day. There was no harm to it. That night he had called for the players to eat together, their last night indeed until the eve of the match when they would be able to dine alone. Woosnam was in splendid spirits. He had travelled to St Andrews in his private plane from Düsseldorf, where he had won the German Open in a sudden-death play-off against another team-mate, Eric Brown. Woosnam had not had a good year and Jacklin had thought long and hard before selecting him as one of his two choices at the expense of another Welshman, Rees. Jacklin's consolation to the latter was, of course, the vice-captain's role, and he had been delighted when Rees had accepted with equanimity. He was even more delighted with Woosnam's return to form, and felt vindicated after some pretty hurtful headlines had greeted the news of his two selections a fortnight earlier. The Irish press, in particular, had been outraged that the claims of Fred Daly and Harry Bradshaw had been overlooked. But it was Rees who had presented Jacklin with a greater dilemma, and he had found it difficult really to argue with the *Daily Mail*'s comment that the captain had gambled heavily on one Welshman who could be either inspirational or inadequate over another whose consistency would surely have been a terrific asset.

Jacklin had gambled. That was the truth of it. But now, as he looked over to the bar, as the Irishman bought a pint of Guinness for himself and a bitter for his partner, he thought to himself: 'I might just have picked a winning hand. Woosnam was inspired in Germany and if he maintains that form this week then that might just be the factor that turns this match in our favour.'

———————

Hagen slept as the motor cavalcade made its way down deserted streets and the White House receded into the distance. He slept as a couple of power-walking Americans who knew what was going on held up Stars and Stripes flags and waved them at the impressive fleet of limousines. The car windows had darkened glass, which suited the captain just fine at this juncture, but Arnold Palmer wound down the one next to him, and Tony Lema too, and they shouted their thanks at the people who were wishing them luck.

A special check-in facility had been arranged at the airport and the players duly filed through as other passengers wiped the sleep from their eyes and recognized the stars who walked among them. Within minutes the players were safely ensconced in their own private lounge. It afforded a view of the departure gates where rows of planes bound for seemingly every destination one could think of were lined up and baggage was being stowed and fuel loaded.

They did not have to wait very long before being called. Their group was seventy-five strong, the remaining passengers being wealthy supporters of the team who were each paying many thousands of dollars for the privilege of completing the party. All, that is, except one very important passenger who had asked to join at the last minute; an unfortunate soul had been bumped off the flight to make way. But then, his consolation was that he could say that he had been saving his seat for the former President, George Bush. A keen golfer, Bush had been very disappointed not to have made a Ryder Cup during his term of office. Vice-President Dan Quayle had stood in for him during the match at Kiawah Island; there had been a war going on at the time, a war in the Gulf that had nothing to do with the so-called 'war on the shore at Kiawah'. But now he had time on his hands, and the match, after all, was going to be played on the course where he was an honorary member. He chuckled to himself, 'Perhaps I could show one or two of the players some of the lines on the greens.' Hagen went over to greet him. Hagen was in his element: two Presidents in twenty-four hours! 'Come and meet the team,' he said.

The hour had almost touched 9 a.m. before everyone was on board and Concorde was ready, its crew and passengers little expecting the welcome that awaited them from people who had long started to gather at Leuchars on the other side of the Atlantic. The pilot wished them a pleasant flight and that is how it turned out. 'Champagne?', asked the flight attendant. 'Yes please,' said Lema. Hagen looked over towards the man they called Champagne Tony, his soul mate in many respects, and now he wasn't unhappy that he had chosen him ahead of Johnny Miller.

A few rows back, Sam Snead and Lee Trevino were laughing and joking with each other about how two hicks from the sticks could end up crossing the Atlantic on Concorde. 'You know what I thought of St Andrews the first time I went there?', Snead said. 'Sam, everyone knows what you thought of St Andrews', Trevino replied. 'Bobby Jones they made a freeman of the city, whatever that means. You, they almost drove out of town'. Snead protested: 'But it did look like a cow pasture. What was I supposed to say when that pressman asked me what I thought? At least the hotels are better these days. I think I'd have refused Hagen's call if they hadn't learned to put a bathroom in with the bedroom.' Trevino knew this last line was in jest. He hadn't thought much of St Andrews either the first time he had seen it. Watson, of course, was in awe of the place. He had his nose deep in a book: *The St Andrews Opens*.

Hogan was reading the latest issue of *Golf Digest*. The good news as far as he was concerned was that he was on the cover. But it was a small reference, for inevitably the Ryder Cup dominated matters. 'Affray in the Bay' was the headline, and a gorgeous picture of St Andrews Bay had been laid underneath it. Inside, the magazine's editors had really gone to town. At Kiawah Island the team had finished up in the Atlantic Ocean celebrating their victory. Now they were to be seen running along the St Andrews beach, the water splashing their ankles. Of course it wasn't really the players; their heads had been stuck on the bodies of the actors portrayed in a famous photographic still from the movie *Chariots of Fire*, which was filmed there. Hagen had loved it. Hogan, of course, couldn't turn the page quickly enough. He was soon immersed in an instruction sequence that dissected his own, widely admired, swing.

Hogan was sitting next to Gene Sarazen. They hardly spoke a word during the entire flight. Sarazen enjoyed his own company too. He watched Hagen as he entertained everybody and thought about how his relationship with him had changed from hero worship as a boy to acute rivalry as a young man to respect as he entered his mid-thirties and the captain his dotage. They were friends in a way too. Now Sarazen wondered how Hagen, with whom he had played in several Ryder Cups and knew as the master at bringing people together, would manage to bind this team of disparate spirits. He dismissed the thought almost as soon as it arrived. There was plenty of time to worry about such things.

———————

Only a handful of people had given up on the Americans as Concorde began its descent into Leuchars at a few minutes after 6 p.m. Although it was not on the original flight path, the pilot had, nevertheless, taken a slight detour to fly right over the Old Course and the plane tipped its wings in recognition of the momentous week of events that was about to unfold. 'Still looks like a cow pasture to me,' Snead said.

The reception that greeted the visiting team was genuinely moving. The cheers could be heard for miles. People waved and smiled and the team responded with reciprocal gestures. Several of the players wandered over and mingled with the public and signed what would be the first of many autographs during the week.

Another posse of cars awaited them, not quite as grand as those that had escorted them to Concorde but luxurious enough. This was the top-of-the-range model offered by the company whose vehicles were the official cars of the Ryder Cup.

There was not much conversation among the players now. It seemed that they had withdrawn into their own thoughts, of what St Andrews meant to them. For Snead, Lema and Nicklaus it was a return to some of their most inspired moments, for Watson a chance to reflect on how his career as a major championship winner all but came to an end there. In no time at all they were motoring along the A91, past the newest of the courses at St Andrews, the Strathtyrum, before turning left and up towards the entrance of the Old Course Hotel. A haar, a cold sea mist, was beginning to descend over the Old Course as the players alighted, and the temperature was considerably lower than that back in Washington. Their luggage was already in their rooms, having come by regular aircraft. 'I'm glad they've given us all sorts of sweaters,' the Florida resident, Gene Sarazen, said. 'I hope they're ready to give us all sorts of whisky,' Hagen responded. O'Connor and Woosnam had long left the bar, which was now filled with other hotel guests and punters who had begun to descend on St Andrews and who would create a carnival atmosphere in the town before the week was over.

Hagen told his players to relax before meeting at 8 p.m. for an informal dinner at which they would begin their discussions about pairings for the foursomes and fourballs matches.

The hotel had employed two masseuses for each team for the week but several players had, in any case, brought their own. Nick Faldo was now relaxing under the trained hands of his regular masseur. The Open champion was in one of his good moods. He had not played in Germany. He had done a couple of corporate days for two of his sponsors, Bridgestone and Pringle, but other than that it had been a quiet week. He had been able to do some fishing in the stream that ran through the bottom tier of his three-tier garden, which fronted the magnificent mansion that he and his wife Gill had bought in Ascot. Several papers had called requesting interviews. He felt almost obliged to answer the one from the *Daily Express*, since he had a contract with them to write so many articles in a given year. Almost, though, was the operative word.

Faldo showered and prepared to join his colleagues in the Jacklin Room for their informal dinner. Once they had known they were getting the Ryder Cup the Japanese owners of the Old Course Hotel had built an extension, complete with still more conference facilities. Off the main area were two rooms big enough to hold fifty people each in comfort. They had been named in honour of the two captains. Jacklin had requested that on this occasion just the players be present and not their wives. He didn't want his team fragmenting into small cliques. It was bad enough, say, that Faldo couldn't stand either Sandy Lyle or Woosnam, but if their wives were there too, then the Faldos would inevitably gather together with the Gallachers. And so on for the whole team.

This was an important day for Jacklin. He regarded it as the day when he had to get players who spent all their lives treating every other golfer as a competitor attuned to the idea of team golf. He was brilliant at this. He knew he had the players' attention when he spoke. As Woosie entered the room, Jacklin congratulated him on his German Open victory. José Maria Olazabal looked sheepish. Like Faldo, Olazabal had given the Düsseldorf tournament a miss, preferring to spend the time instead in his home adjacent to the 7th fairway of the Royal San Sebastian course where he had grown up. While Faldo had gone fishing, Olazabal had joined his father's hunting party and they had gone up into the hills nearby. Many hours later they had come home with twenty-five grouse, a dozen rabbits, three hares and a couple of ducks.

Olazabal, perhaps not surprisingly, looked a picture of health. Jacklin enjoyed his sense of fun. He liked the way Olazabal's arrogant, haughty air on the course melted almost into shyness when confronted with this type of company. Brown and O'Connor entered, enjoying both a drink and a laugh. 'Nice to see you smiling, Eric,' Jacklin said mischievously.

'Let's hope I'm still smiling when I see your pairings,' Brown replied, half in jest, but with a certain seriousness attached too. Brown had been the second of Jacklin's two selections, and it had been a close-run thing between him and another Scot with a similarly tempestuous nature, Colin Montgomerie. What had told against the latter was the fact that Jacklin had wanted to pair Faldo with Peter Oosterhuis rather than Montgomerie. That had meant it had come down to who would be the better singles player, and Brown's record and demeanour in such matches were beyond argument. Jacklin had come in for some stick here too, from some of the golf correspondents who enjoyed Montgomerie's candour if not some of his more boorish behavioural patterns. But it was not a decision that had led to any sleepless nights for the captain. The only difference was that where Montgomerie was often charming company off the course, Brown was often not.

Sandy Lyle was the last to enter. He had gone to the Hagen

Room by mistake. 'That's the big Lil we know and love', Jacklin sighed.

'You'll be glad I did when you hear what I've got to say,' Lyle responded. 'When I opened the door the Americans were engaged in a full-blown row!'

––––––––––

Indeed they were. Sarazen's worst fears were already materializing. Lyle had made his grand entrance just as Palmer was pointing the finger and refusing flat out to play with Jack Nicklaus. 'But the Europeans will be so intimidated by the sight of Jack 'n' Arnie they'll be two down before they start,' Hagen reasoned.

'You can't get round us with flattery,' the pair said in unison.

'Sorry for butting in,' said Lyle. For a few moments, as Lyle skipped hurriedly away, there was silence and some embarrassment, for the unscheduled entrance of one of the opposition had taken away some of the heat from the incident. It was as if seeing the opposing player had concentrated their resolve. They started to chatter away among themselves. Hagen was thinking: 'I have the greatest collection of players the world has ever seen and yet I'm struggling to make them a team.' He decided it was time for a grand gesture of his own. No glib words. This time it would come from the heart. He said: 'If the Ryder Cup was a stroke play event we'd all be in the dining room, with our chosen companions, and then we'd go out and play seventy-two holes and I have no doubt that eight of you gentlemen in this room would finish in the top ten. Yet if we continue to behave like this we will not win this contest. Our trip will have been in vain. Do any of you seriously want to be on a losing Ryder Cup side at the Home of Golf? For I'll tell you this: I don't want to be a losing captain. And I'm quite prepared to embarrass any member of this team in the press who wilfully, by his actions, leads to the likelihood of this happening.'

The players were stunned. Hogan was impressed, despite himself. The captain had finally acted like one, he thought. A moment's silence descended. Who would speak? Hagen knew who would break the ice. The iceman himself, and there were times when he was glad to have him on board. 'Put me with Nicklaus. We'll beat anyone,' Hogan said, with characteristically clipped tones.

'Put me with Palmer,' Sarazen added. 'We'll make a good team.

It'll be my accuracy and his swashbuckling talents. Walter, it used to work when you and I were partners. It can work again.' Hagen, in fact, had wanted to put Sarazen with Lema but he liked the ideas he was hearing from the floor. Most of all he liked the restoration of bonhomie. He agreed to both pairings.

He asked Watson to play with Byron Nelson, a mutual admiration society if ever there was one. The captain knew that Nelson would agree to anything he asked of him. He thought back to the first time the pair had met, in the US PGA Championship in Dallas, when Hagen had been dazzled by the Texan sunlight. He asked his caddy to run ahead, to get him a cap, when the 11-year-old Byron Nelson had stepped forward: 'Please sir, you can have mine.' Nelson's mother, it was, who reminded Hagen of the incident when her son had qualified all these years later for the Ryder Cup. 'You're not going to ask me for the cap back, are you?', Hagen had said to her, laughing.

'Lee, I want you to go with Billy', Hagen said, returning to the present.

Trevino liked the idea of partnering Billy Casper. 'We'll be nicknamed the fat bellies!', Trevino said. Hagen's theory in this instance was that Casper's dour nature would stop Trevino from getting carried away. Trevino had a wonderful rapport with the British galleries. But Hagen wanted him to concentrate when the games were on and he knew that the sight of the unsmiling Mormon next to him would curb some of Trevino's excesses.

One pairing had been decided before they had entered the room, before they had even boarded Concorde. Snead was going to play with Lloyd Mangrum, the dapper Texan with his trim moustache and trendy hairstyle. Mangrum had said little up to this point, but everyone knew he was there, for his cigarette smoke circled the room. They had been in the place an hour and already he had filled his ashtray with thirty butts. He was even a couple ahead in this respect of Hagen himself, the team's other chain smoker. It was easy to mistake this as a sign of nervousness but Hagen hadn't hesitated in making Mangrum one of his selections, for he knew the value of his partnership with Snead. The pair just hit it off from the first time they played Ryder Cup golf together. Europe had Olazabal and Ballesteros; America had Mangrum and Snead. Heaven knows what would happen if they were ever drawn to meet each other.

By a process of elimination, then, Tom Kite would play with Lema. This bothered neither player. Lema was just happy to be back at St Andrews, and would have partnered Tom Cobbleigh, let alone Tom Kite, if that was what his captain wanted. But the partnership made sense in any case. Lema, in winning an Open over the Old Course, had shown that he could play this famous old links. Kite, in several previous skirmishes, had fully demonstrated that he could play Ryder Cup golf.

And so it was settled. The bickering had ended. The players were almost ashamed of the earlier scene. 'Forget it all,' Hagen said, a man who never held a grievance in his life. 'Let's eat,' he added, but thoughts of food were interrupted by a knock on the door. No, it wasn't Sandy Lyle still struggling to find his way. It was former President Bush.

'Hope you don't mind the intrusion. I've just had dinner with the captain of the Royal and Ancient, and I just wanted to know how it was going.' Forced smiles suddenly greeted him from everywhere.

'It's going just fine, Georgie,' said Hagen, who knew how to make a President feel one of the crowd.

'Well, I've got some business to see to for the next two days or so but I'll be around for the official dinner on Wednesday night, so I'll see you all then,' he said, and left.

A minute later, another knock at the door. This time it was the Americans' catering crew for the week and they brought just what the team had ordered: sandwiches of fifty-seven varieties. Suddenly, Hagen wasn't hungry. The forced smile was gone. He poured himself a large Black Bush whiskey from the mobile bar that had been set up in the corner of the room, and added a drop of water.

'Really?', said Jacklin to Lyle. 'Still, a bit of a dumb decision anyway. Who would ever put Nicklaus with Palmer? Everyone knows they're not happy in each other's company.'

'A bit like putting me with Faldo, really,' Lyle said.

Jacklin gave a rueful grin. 'Yes, thank you Sandy!'

Jacklin wanted the team to eat before they began any conversation about pairings. For one thing, he knew this session would not be anywhere near as acrimonious as that of the Americans, for most of his players naturally paired up. For another, he wanted to get them relaxed in each other's company before he started firing bullets. The table was of an oval shape, though large enough to sit fourteen people. The meal was a two-course affair: a Stilton soup was followed by a fish pie. Faldo had an extra course: a large piece of gateau. 'I don't know how you're not twenty stone,' Brian Barnes said.

Faldo chortled, 'Jealous, by any chance, are we?' Faldo was so pleased with this remark that he decided to have some cheese as well.

Ballesteros was keen to talk about Barcelona's victory in the opening match of the Champions' League against Rangers but none of the Scots were taking the bait. Actually, Brown and Gallacher were too busy talking about the forthcoming Edinburgh derby that was due to be played at Easter Road on the Saturday of the Ryder Cup. Neither was particularly upset at Rangers' loss. The commentators could pretend until kingdom come that a victory for such and such a home club was a great result for British football but Brown and Gallacher cared about their clubs and them alone, and since they followed Edinburgh teams they were almost pleased at the Glasgow side's defeat. 'Great goal by Romario, no?', Ballesteros said.

'We could certainly do with him against Hibs,' Brown, an unswerving follower of Hearts' cause, said.

'More chance of seeing Romeo,' Gallacher, a Hibernian man, replied.

Bernhard Langer, another keen football fan, was desperately trying to make his mark on this conversation but O'Connor was rabbiting in his ear and the impenetrable Irish accent and the fact he wasn't paying close attention anyway meant the German was making out only about every fourth word. 'Afraid' . . . 'up' . . . 'in' . . . 'smoke', were the words he caught. He glanced around at O'Connor, who was giving him his best pleading look. Langer didn't know what to say. What was going up in smoke? The team's chances? The room? Langer didn't like to ask him to repeat the question. He tried his 'whatever you say' facial expression, and was showered with O'Connor's grateful thanks. In fact, O'Connor had said: 'I'm afraid I'm going to have to light up in this room and have a smoke,' and he had asked Langer because Langer had requested of Jacklin that smoking be banned from this gathering place. Langer realized that this was one battle that he wasn't going to win, but he did ask O'Connor to leave the table while he had his smoke. At least that way he could talk football in peace.

Next to him was the giant figure of Peter Oosterhuis, who had come back from a struggling season on the US tour to qualify by right for the team. Though Oosty and Jacklin were far from being close friends — they had enjoyed too much of a rivalry in their heyday for them ever to be close friends — the latter was nevertheless glad to have Oosterhuis on the team. Jacklin admired the way that Oosterhuis, though able to do nothing against the Americans when playing in a stroke play event, could yet have the strength of will to dismiss all known form and beat the same players come the Ryder Cup. He had done this time and again, and Jacklin had no doubt that he would do so again this week.

Now Barnes's booming voice was dominating conversation. He knew that this would be the last evening on which he could have a few beers without Jacklin having a word in his ear asking him to slow down. 'Me and Bernard. We'll take on anything the Americans care to throw at us. We'll take them all on at the same time if necessary.' Jacklin groaned. He could see Barnes was going to make his usual contribution to the proceedings. Jacklin looked around the table. He noted the way many of the players were talking to the men who would be their course partners for most of the week. There were times when the captain's job was made to look very easy.

He stood up. 'Gentleman, our own answer to Inspector Clouseau has reported that the American team are bickering among themselves. I forecast that this will continue until the final day. Nicklaus can't stand Palmer. Palmer can't stand Hogan. Hogan can't stand Hagen. Hagen doesn't understand Nelson. Nelson doesn't understand Trevino. And so on. We may have our differences too but they seem minimal when compared to this team of individuals. Just remember that however talented they are, the Ryder Cup is a team game and team spirit is all-important, and this is the vital ingredient we have in our favour. Gentleman, most of the pairings that I'm about to announce will hardly come as a surprise. Barnesy, after your little outburst it will come as some relief for you to know that I intend putting you out with Bernard. Similarly, Nick, you will play with Oosty. Seve and Ollie, what can I say? These three pairings I'd like to think are cast in stone and will serve us well over the first two days. You all know each other well, you've all shown you can do it in Ryder Cup competition. I know the Americans are fond of singing the praises of Lloyd and Sam but I think you would all beat even that formidable pairing given a fair run of the ball.

'For the other three pairings I'm open to ideas and how the players concerned are playing in the four days leading up to the match. Obviously, on the Friday morning, I want all guns blazing and I want the eight players who are in the best form to play. Dai has suggested that we try out Henry and Bernhard over the first couple of practice days and I am not averse to that. I think Woosie and Himself should play together too. Which leaves, ah, Sandy and Eric.'

Jacklin sat down. Eric Brown stood up. 'Are you bloody serious?', he said. 'Me and Sandy? Me and bloody Sandy Lyle?' Believe it or not, this was Brown's idea of tact. If he'd fully vented his spleen he'd have said: 'Here I am, a full-blooded Scot, who is fired up by the thrill and chase of the Ryder Cup and here you are, Jacklin, putting me out with a man who sometimes plays as if he doesn't care what day it is.' 'Opposites attract, sometimes, Eric, haven't you heard that?', Jacklin tried weakly.

'Well, I'm game if Eric's game,' said Sandy.

'I'm not bloody game. No offence, Sandy,' Brown said.

The problem for Brown was that everyone else thought the pairings splendid. Cotton and Langer had both struggled manfully over the years with putting difficulties but each totally admired the way the other had coped. If these two were intense, then O'Connor, or Himself as he was known to all and sundry, and Woosnam would make a more relaxed combination. At the bar earlier they had predicted that they would be teamed up and now here was the confirmation.

Brown was still holding out. He wouldn't have minded partnering Langer, or Faldo, or at least someone with a little fire in their belly. Even the Hibs supporter would have been all right. Brown knew Gallacher was a fighter. But Lyle? Someone who gave up all too readily? Well, Lyle had better be sure about one thing. If he gave up in any match in which he was a partner of Brown's then he would not be forgiven. Which was, of course, the way Jacklin had worked the thing out all along. He was hoping Brown would so intimidate his partner that the brilliantly talented but frustratingly lackadaisical Lyle would be focused enough to produce his very best golf.

———————

The two captains had agreed to meet at 10 p.m. to offer platitudes to one another. 'Clever move, sending Sandy to our room,' said Hagen, as the pair shook hands in the privacy of a suite that had been reserved expressly for just such an occasion. 'If only,' laughed Jacklin. 'You know Sandy,' and Hagen laughed too. He knew that there was no plot involved. He knew Sandy had once taken a wrong turning on a Florida interstate highway and driven for 120 miles before spotting that something was wrong. He knew Sandy had once won a tournament sponsored by a Japanese whisky firm and then stood up and thanked the Chinese sponsors. He knew that Sandy had once been asked to rate his golf on a scale of one to ten and had replied: 'Six out of ten, or 70 per cent.' Sandy Lyle was more than capable of going to the wrong room.

Hagen congratulated Jacklin on his successes on the US Senior tour. Jacklin congratulated Hagen on his Hollywood film career, which had precluded him from playing in all but a handful of Senior events. How it had started was a story oft told: with his playing the lead role in the golf-related movie *Fields of Greens*, before branching out far beyond the realms of sport. Indeed, Hagen was as natural at this new career as his first profession. The easy charm and grace with which he captivated the First Lady had smoothly translated itself on to the silver screen, and although now in his mid-fifties and overweight he retained some of his raffish good looks. If the studios wanted an American Sean Connery then Hagen, invariably, was the man they sought. This new path did lead some to wonder how on earth he could be selected as captain. Hogan, for a start, disliked him for this direction. Not out of jealousy; he simply could not understand how someone so talented at golf could not want to work at it continuously. Hogan, it had to be remembered, often had to be dragged kicking and screaming from the practice ground. Hagen thought it merely a place where one warmed up. The American, though, was widely regarded as the best at the job. With Jacklin, there had been even less debate. Both were still considerable players, of course: Hagen, so adept at the wiles and cruel fates of match play, with an ability to shrug off the excesses of poor fortune; Jacklin, to whom no one was unbeatable if the mood was upon him. Now they faced each other on a plush leather sofa, the room otherwise empty of people. They had one final drink. Even Hagen was tired. Usually, the adrenalin was pumping at this time and it would keep him going until the early hours. But it had been one hell of a day: the photoshoot, the flight, the row, and all on ninety minutes' sleep. Jacklin could see he was fading. He was fading too.

Both would enhance the occasion of this Ryder Cup considerably with their charisma, their candour, their humour and, most of all, their inspiration. But that was in the future. For now they enquired of each other's health and their respective journeys to St Andrews, and wished each other good luck for the toil that lay ahead.

2

Tuesday:
Settling In

THE AMERICAN PLAYERS filed into the Hagen Room for a 7.30 a.m. breakfast. The kitchen staff at the Old Course Hotel were prepared: there was corned beef hash; grits; biscuits and gravy; and quite a few things that wouldn't normally have found their way on to a St Andrews breakfast menu.

Hogan was first down, then Palmer. Both ordered a substantial meal. Both looked out of the window on to the 17th hole but they couldn't see very far. The haar hadn't lifted. Indeed, they would be very lucky if it had gone in time for the first American practice round at 9.30 a.m. Palmer said as much to Hogan. Hogan said: 'I'm not playing anyway.'

Palmer's bottom jaw almost touched the floor. Hogan not playing? There weren't many things that caused him to stop in his tracks but this was as unlikely as Hagen going a night without a drop of Scotch. 'Does Walter know?', Palmer asked. 'He knows', Hogan replied.

'What's up, then? Are you ill? Are your legs bothering you?' Palmer knew he shouldn't have asked all these questions of Hogan. The great man never referred to the aftermath of the car crash that almost cost him his life. Palmer knew that he had played many rounds in a lot of pain from the legs that had to be rebuilt with pins and plates but Hogan never admitted it, never gave in. 'Are you captain or something now, Arnold? I didn't realize I had to answer to you too.'

It hardly satisfied Palmer's curiosity. It hardly prompted more conversation between them. Palmer was delighted when the other players began to file in, thus breaking the tension. Watson's face was beaming. 'A Scotch mist,' he said, looking towards the 17th. 'Don't you just love all the different possibilities that playing links golf conjures up?'

Mangrum lit a cigarette. He joined Snead, who was enjoying the heartiest breakfast of all. 'This isn't a bad hotel, you know, Lloyd,' Snead said. 'Certainly better than the pigsty I stayed in first time I came here.' Mangrum laughed to himself: the course was a cow pasture and the hotel a pigsty. There's only one Sam Snead.

Hagen came in, looking a great deal healthier than at this time the previous day in America. He took an orange juice from the table and, ordering himself a cup of coffee and some toast, took a light from Mangrum's cigarette and set the scene for the day's events.

'Gentlemen, we are first on the tee for practice today, and that is at 9.30 a.m. Before that we have a photosession for the benefit of our clothing sponsors and then another with the press. As you know, our colour is red sweaters and shirts today, with blue slacks. Your caddies have already been given the golf bags for this week and they will obviously take care of your clubs.

'I don't think we want to give too much away to the enemy this early in the week so I don't plan for us to go out in entirely the formations that we talked about last evening. It makes sense for Lloyd and Sam to play with other people, since they know each other's games so well anyway, and also Tom and Byron since there will be no separating them during the match unless one falls totally out of form.

'Gentlemen, I suggest that we play nine holes of alternate shots and nine holes of fourballs, and of course you're allowed to have side-bets. In fact, I encourage side-bets. There will be an overall bet too, and the team with the lowest score will walk off with the money. I suggest each of us puts in $50. Oh, I shall be playing with Jack today as Ben has asked to be excused practice for the day. We'll meet again here at 2 p.m.'

So. They were still none the wiser. Now everyone was curious. What was wrong with Ben? The news, as news does, started to spread quickly, and by the time Hagen would address the press in the first of his conferences at 3 p.m., everyone knew what the opening question would be.

———————

The haar was not thick enough to prevent Jacklin going on his morning walk. This was something that he had built into his routine in recent years. It had begun in Scotland when he used to walk his dogs on the heath that surrounded the lovely home which he and Astrid had shared for two short years. It had continued when they moved to Palm Beach, and now he walked on more sand, albeit where the temperature was many degrees cooler.

Jacklin loved this time of day. The beach was deserted. The corporate village was silent. The wind blew gently and the sea spilled out quietly on to the sand. Given what had happened to the world during the past five hundred years, it was amazing how little had changed here.

A couple of keen joggers suddenly appeared out of the mist and shouted a cheery good morning, little knowing the identity of the man they had just passed. Jacklin saw a pebble in the sand that was not unlike a golf ball in shape and size. He stood next to it and addressed it as he would if it were a ball. He played an imaginary shot and chuckled to himself: another imperious drive. He picked up the pebble and cast it out to sea. 'For luck,' he said, aloud.

And then another jogger. This time, as the seemingly obligatory morning greeting was being prepared by both parties a look of recognition fell on their faces. 'Hi, Tony, so good to see you again,' Tom Kite said.

'What the hell are you doing running in this stuff?', Jacklin replied.

'It's not so bad,' responded Kite.

Jacklin had always been a great admirer of Kite. In truth he was not one of the more popular American players in Britain. Many golfing folk felt the smile that usually accompanied his every move smacked a little too much of insincerity. Jacklin knew that the truth was rather different.

'You're sure earning some money on the Senior tour. That's a hell of a comeback,' Kite said.

'Tom, it's been the best thing that's happened to me profession-ally for a decade. I've had a rough time. It's been great to free myself of some bad business deals. It's a load off my mind. How's Christy?'

'She's fine. She's not a great fan of this weather. I like the change. I'm getting used to it here at this time having played in the Dunhill Cup.'

'To be honest I'm with your wife on this one. The years in Florida have thinned my blood. Anyway, you don't want to stop too long. You don't want to get a chill. I'd like you to get a chill, but . . .'

Kite smiled. 'Have a good week. Just lose, OK.'

And with that the bespectacled Texan replaced the scarf across his mouth. Now only his forehead was exposed to the elements. He looked something of a ridiculous sight, Jacklin laughed to himself, but now he returned to his own thoughts, and looked at his watch. Seven a.m. Better be getting back.

Two eggs, three rashers of bacon, four sausages and five slices of toast had given Faldo some appetite for golf. He was on the practice range at 8.30 a.m., and next to him, amazingly, was Lyle. Perhaps the thought of partnering Brown really was going to frighten him into his best golf.

This was a time reserved for the Americans to practise but they didn't mind the two strangers in their midst. They were just finishing up anyway. Most came over and either shook hands or nodded a welcome. Lyle was one of the most popular players on the American tour. 'You come to our room last night and now you want to practise with us. I'm sorry, Sandy, but it's time you were told: there are no vacancies and you don't qualify anyway to be on our team,' Sandy's great friend, Trevino, said.

Even Faldo looked up from what he was doing and smiled. 'Anyone get any fog lamps?', he said.

The American photoshoot went reasonably smoothly. All the players knew that this was the acceptable face of commercialism. It was a chore but a necessary one. Ashworth had been good to them all. Part of the deal was that every player would get several layers of cashmere clothing for each day. Hagen got some monogrammed silk shirts.

The players stood behind their golf bags; they posed without their golf bags; they put on their rainwear equipment ('No point taking it off, is there?', quipped Snead); and then the press photographic battalion marched on to the scene.

Of course the press didn't just want studio shots; they tried to get individual photos as well. The man from the *Sun*, complete with sombrero in hand, approached Trevino and asked him for a posed photo. Trevino gave a two-word answer that left the photographer in no doubt that his request had been turned down.

It all took about forty-five minutes and when it was over the Americans were ready to play. They climbed into chauffeur-driven cars for the short journey to the course. Down Pilmour Links before turning left into Golf Place. Past the golf stores on the left and the magnificent small bookshop, Quarto, which didn't just specialize in tomes about the sport. And then the course itself, though it could not be seen for the large grandstand that had been built behind the final green.

The cars pulled up outside the magnificent building that served as the clubhouse for the Royal and Ancient Golf Club of St Andrews. Quite a crowd had gathered and they clapped warmly as the players smiled and made their way into the clubhouse and then down the stairs into the locker room. Their quarters, so to speak, were on the left, and while changing their shoes a couple of the players wore wry smiles as they read a couple of Roy Ullyett cartoons that adorned the walls.

Back out they came, to more applause, for even at this hour the 18th was lined with people and the grandstand was half full. The players wore large smiles and joked with one another. A couple of the wisecracks were not even forced ones for the benefit of the cameras.

The members, settled in their armchairs, leaned forward a little to see who would strike the first blow. There were Nicklaus, Lema, Trevino and Hagen. There were quite a few gasps all around when it became clear that Hagen was not there just to wish his men well as they began their opening practice round. He was going to hit first!

'He's quite a showboat, isn't he?', said one member in the snug comfort of the main lounge, which affords a wonderful view of the opening hole. But Hagen wasn't showboating. This wasn't a ceremonial drive. And as he struck the ball unerringly straight with his characteristically freewheeling style, and as his three partners followed him in turn, it dawned on everyone who witnessed this little scene that Hagen was going to play and that one of the American players was missing.

The man from the Press Association counted them all out and when they had left the opening hole he ran back to the media tent and filed his story: 'Hogan's Mystery Absence'. The news spread like a forest fire among the journalists, who as ever, on the first of three preview days, were wondering what the hell they were supposed to write about. At least that problem was solved. Now it became a quest to find out what had happened to Hogan. Was he ill? Were his legs playing up? The questions that Palmer had rattled off two hours previously were now being repeated by a chorus of inquisitive hacks.

The truth of the matter was a little less prosaic. Hogan was not ill. His legs felt fine. Indeed, he was feeling better than for some years. It was just that he had a little business to attend to, a few memories to rekindle.

And so the chauffeured car met him at the completion of the photoshoot and off he headed in the direction of Dundee. On the other side of the Tay Bridge, they picked up the first signs for their ultimate destination: Carnoustie. Hogan couldn't come all this way and not see once more the course that meant so much to him, a course that he felt was so much better in every way than the one where the Ryder Cup was being staged. It would be a visit that would sum up the man: without show and without fanfare.

Like many an American before him, Hogan was not impressed upon his first viewing of Carnoustie. He thought the setting dull, which, undeniably, it is. He didn't like the rock-hard fairways either, and some of the bunkering he considered stupid, and most of the holes made little sense. It was in rank bad condition, or so he thought, and it was all so simple and aesthetically displeasing to the eye. That was his first impression, and it was one that didn't leave him for some time when he got home.

The difference between Hogan and most of his compatriots was that he didn't give in to this deceiving appearance. He had played the course several times in practice and by the time the Open began, the one that he would go on to win, he was familiar with its subtle tests.

But a few weeks after he had returned home he realized that he hadn't stopped thinking about Carnoustie. One morning he woke with a start and he realized in that instant what the course had been all about. And he fell in love with the place right there and then; it was in his bones. Years later he told a reporter from the local *Fort Worth Star Telegram* that no course and no event ever gave him greater pleasure – which was a far cry from what he had said at the time.

Now here he was, years older and back for a reunion of the soul and of the heart. He stepped on to the first tee and thought of those great days, how he had improved in every round, how he had got to the stage that by the final day he felt he could have shot any score that it took to win. Now the feeling of inspiration returned, as he had wanted in the week of the Ryder Cup. This was why Hagen had been more than prepared to countenance a day's leave of absence.

Hogan's first drive pitched on the bank of the shelf known popularly as the elephant's graveyard and his blind second shot to the opening green finished 18 ft from the flag and the putt by the hole's side. This was the sort of golf that Hogan was known for and this was how it would be on this day. There was hardly a drive that strayed from the middle of the fairway unless he wanted it to; hardly an iron shot missed the green. At the 5th, where Frank Sinatra had momentarily disturbed his concentration by waving a greeting, he replayed the chip he had left himself on the final day of the Open. He imagined the pin where it had been on that day, and this time his chip shot fell 10 ft past, whereas on the day it had gone in. He still holed the putt for par. At the 6th he once more chose the tiger line, just as he had on all four days of the Open. Aiming at the out of bounds, Hogan once more hit the power fade that brought his ball back to the narrow strip of fairway between the bunkers and the fence. He was sitting pretty, once more, in Hogan's Alley.

On a day free of the haar that still clung to the perimeter of St Andrews, with just the slightest of breezes for company, Hogan plucked five birdies from Carnoustie and didn't give a single stroke back. He was round in 67, although he wasn't totally satisfied. He had had many chances for birdies and had left many putts short. 'The greens are still in need of a good lawnmower, just as they were back then,' he said to himself. But any displeasure soon evaporated. Even Hogan had to recognize that a 67 was still some score at Carnoustie even without a strong wind. He thought back to his Open victory: he had shot 73, 71, 70, 68. And now a

67. 'Now I'm ready for St Andrews,' he thought. He left as unheralded as he had arrived. True, a couple of keen golfers had recognized him as he began his journey of renewal and had followed him, but they never spoke to him and neither did he to them. They didn't clap any of his strokes but watched in awe both his power and his accuracy. When it was over, that awe was still with them, and they were powerless to request an autograph. By the time they had recovered their ability to speak Hogan had gone, back to the Old Course, and back to reality.

Where all hell had broken loose. The media tent was buzzing with intrigue. Hogan wasn't in the hotel: where was he then? Hagen wasn't saying anything. A couple of journalists had followed him out on to the course. They caught up with him on the 4th hole and asked him the question. Hagen was at his most teasingly infuriating. 'Gentlemen, how are you? Don't you know you shouldn't disturb a golfer as he goes about his business? Surely you do. How long have you been doing this job now? Jim, what is it, eighteen years? Would you like me to fire questions at you as you're writing your stories? Now, please, give us a little time and space. I'll reveal all at the press conference.'

Hagen read their minds. 'And don't bother asking any of the other players,' he said. 'They don't know.' With that he turned away, giggling loudly to himself. He loved the idea that they were calling him every name under the sun and he loved too the thought that the whole press tent was wondering what had happened to Hogan. He liked, also, the idea of the Europeans knowing, and wondered if conjectural thoughts might be entering their minds when they should be concentrating on the job in hand.

With this to think about, Hagen enjoyed himself hugely. He played very well, too – better indeed than his three playing partners, which might have been worrying but for the fact that this was Tuesday and the contest, in golfing terms, was still years away.

Hagen loved to watch Nicklaus at close quarters. He could see that Nicklaus wasn't properly focused yet. Three practice rounds was an inordinate amount for him and particularly on a course where he knew practically every hump and hollow. Hagen admired his great strength and his even greater will. He had seen it at the 9th, a gentle par 4 of 356 yards and, with the breeze coming from the west, as it was on this day, an eminently birdieable hole. They were all square against Lema and Trevino. Although all four had driven from the first, they were now, as Hagen had requested, playing foursomes golf, and it was Nicklaus's turn to drive.

Hagen could see the determination writ large. For eight holes he had been cruising. Now there was a little bit of pressure on. He had no doubts what would happen next. Nicklaus chose a no. 3 wood and gave the ball plenty of air. It sailed on the wind, as effortlessly as if it had possessed wings, before falling 20 yards short of the green and then bouncing, bounding, skipping, rolling to 12 ft from the hole. 'That's my boy,' Hagen said proudly.

'That's just not fair, Jack,' Trevino said, at the top of his backswing as he attempted a golfing reply. It was a good drive, but Lema's chip meant that Trevino was putting for birdie before Hagen was putting for eagle. Trevino missed. Hagen couldn't stop laughing but it didn't stop him holing the putt. Few things stopped Hagen holing putts. Even at this advanced stage in his life he remained supreme on the greens and especially on occasions like this where the pressure was merely self-induced.

The pair won the back nine as well. Hagen had four birdies over that stretch and hit the ball so well that Lema said he thought he should be a playing captain. Lema marvelled at his captain's wide stance and how open he was as he addressed a putt. He took the putter head considerably inside the line. But how could you argue when he holed out so regularly? How could you argue when you were being soundly beaten? As they approached the final green, Hagen could see the journalists gathered on the path in front of the clubhouse. He hadn't finished teasing them yet. 'Surely you can't be in that much of a hurry,' he said. 'Look, I want to watch my fellows play a few shots and then have a quick chat with them and then I'll be with you. OK?'

'No, it's not bloody OK,' a journalist with an evening newspaper deadline muttered under his breath. But Hagen was the ultimate charmer.

'Fine,' they said.

American faces were beaming as they came down the final fairway. There were certainly some very good shots played. Palmer drove almost to the front of the green and then putted up through the Valley of Sin to 'gimme' length. Gene Sarazen, his partner, squealed his delight, for it gave them a 1-hole victory over Billy Casper and Lloyd Mangrum.

Hagen's intention may have been to split Watson and Nelson for the day's practice but it hadn't worked out that way. They were still together. On the practice ground, Watson had been watched over by his mentor and it just felt right that they should be partners on the course. 'Byron, I'd just like you to keep an eye out for this odd swing that produces a hook,' Watson said.

That wasn't the problem on the 17th, where, after the perfect drive, Watson had hit his second shot over the green and over the road and almost against the boundary wall. How the photographers loved that one, as the parallels with what happened when he lost the Open there to Severiano Ballesteros were all too obvious.

'Go exorcize some demons, Tom,' Nelson said. Watson chipped up to 10 ft and missed the putt. His partner saved him. Nelson, safely on the front of the green in 2, got his par to give them a 2 and 1 victory over Sam Snead and Tom Kite.

Snead was less than happy at having to hand over some money. He offered a double or quits bet down the last. It was accepted. Snead's drive was every bit as long as Palmer's but the birdie he too went on to acquire was matched by one from Watson.

Hagen enjoyed watching this friendly rivalry among his players. They may not all get on in a room together but put them out on a course and he could see his plans coming together, as their own skills and their respect for those of each other made for a potent combination.

The American team adjourned for lunch. A thick vegetable soup was the most popular choice, as might be expected on a day that had been chilly though bright, and pleasant enough once the sun had burned off the haar. Hagen stood up. 'Gentlemen, I'm sorry I was a bit vague this morning about Ben. There's no problem with him playing. He just wanted the day off to go and play Carnoustie and I saw nothing wrong with that. I didn't want to tell you because I knew the press would bother you if you knew.

'On to the golf. Jack and I shot 34 for the front side in alternate shots and 30 for the back side in fourballs. Anyone beat that? No? Ah, what a shame. Looks like the money's all ours, Jack.' Hogan entered the room. He nodded a greeting to Hagen and ordered his own soup.

'How'd it go?', Snead asked.

Hogan was almost moved to tears. 'It was great,' he said. 'It was simply great.'

Hagen strode into the media tent just five minutes after the appointed hour. It was standing room only, even though the interview room had been built to seat two hundred people. When asked what he would like to drink he smiled and said: 'Scotch and water.' He settled for a Coke from the wide selection of soft drinks available in the fridge nearby. As he poured it into a cup, the questions began.

The press officer opened up by asking for a statement about Hogan, and the American captain explained the mystery in a couple of short sentences. 'Bang go a couple of back-page leads, I guess,' Hagen said, and a few writers could not stop themselves nodding in agreement.

'How was meeting the President?'

'Which one?', Hagen laughed. He knew which one. Hagen thought to himself: 'Well, he turned out to be quite a dude and his wife quite a babe and we had this real close dance while he played the saxophone . . .' 'It was just great,' he said. 'It was a quiet dinner and he wished us good luck and told us not to bother coming back if we didn't bring the cup back as well.'

Hagen was asked about the form of his players and he replied as he would have done even if it were not the truth: they were all playing well. It was anodyne stuff. He was asked about the galleries; he praised the galleries. 'The Scottish galleries are among the most knowledgeable anywhere and they won't believe all that the more excited among you will write,' Hagen said, winking at one of the American journalists. He was asked about the hype; he said he thought it inevitable given the stature of the contest and the ability in each team. But he did not believe it had got or would get out of hand. He repeated what he had said in several magazine interviews, that he thought the match would be a testament to sportsmanship, and a world away, for example, from the poisoned atmosphere that had been present in the build-up to the match at Kiawah Island.

Then came the bombshell. 'Could you please tell us about the row on Monday night and whether you think it will affect morale?' Hagen looked stunned for a moment. He had sat there for half an hour batting back formal questions and now here was a real test of his diplomatic skills. He thought about bluffing it out and saying 'What row?', but eventually decided on another tack. 'Call that a row?', he parried.

The questioner persisted: 'I understand there was a disagreement, then, between Jack and Arnold and they impressed strongly upon you that there was no way they were going to partner each other.'

Hagen replied that it was ridiculous to interpret such discussions even as a disagreement, let alone a row. He then added simply: 'Jack and Arnold are quite happy to play together and may well end up playing together but you'll have to wait until Thursday afternoon to find that out.'

The American captain breathed deeply and waited for another follow-up. 'You can say quite categorically that it wasn't a row, then?'

'Yes, I categorically can,' Hagen said.

And then a question about whether he was settled in his own mind about who would play with whom. He answered affirmatively.

He was asked once more about his two selections, and spoke of the merits of Mangrum and Lema. 'They were very hard decisions to make, among the hardest of my career. I thought about Raymond Floyd. I thought about Johnny Miller. I thought about Gene Littler, and Paul Azinger, and how do you leave out Jimmy Demaret, who has never lost in the Ryder Cup?

'But I felt I had to pick Lloyd because he's a great alternate shot and fourballs player and in particular he dovetails so well with Sam Snead. There's a bit of information for you fellas. Sam will play with Lloyd.'

After the gentle laughter had subsided, Hagen continued: 'I also felt that Tony's experience of winning the Open at St Andrews gave him the nod over Raymond's fighting qualities. Tony's a great team player too. You asked about a row. No one could have a row when Lema's around.'

Nevertheless, Hagen knew that the so-called row was now going to dominate headlines and decided to do something about neutralizing them. He said: 'I think this is the strongest American side that has ever come to these shores and I think we will continue this run of success we have had recently. American golf is enjoying a halcyon period, and while I respect Tony Jacklin and the strong European side that has gathered here, I still can't see any other result than an American victory.'

The interview over, Hagen said that he would return the following afternoon with his team, who would be available to answer questions. He added that this would be the only occasion that such a privilege would be extended, although if individual players were happy to speak to the press after the conclusion of their matches then he had no objections.

Hagen's unruffled expression left him the moment he departed the media tent. He was furious. How on earth had information about the row leaked out? Then he remembered the impromptu entrance of Sandy Lyle.

Actually, poor Lyle had never mentioned the incident to anyone from the press. He had related it to his caddie, who had then told a journalist. Lyle had other things on his mind. Like a troubling hook that surfaced whenever he tried to hit a big drive. Like playing with Eric Brown.

Jacklin saw no reason to indulge in any kidology on the first full practice day. He thought his pairings rather chose themselves and so the players went out with the partners they would almost certainly still have when the phoney war ended.

It was a mixed bag. Barnes played poorly but then it was still far too early in the week for him. Woosnam clearly remained on a high after his German Open win and struggled to concentrate. Faldo asked to be excused after nine holes, saying it would be more beneficial for him to spend the time on the practice ground.

But Oosterhuis struck the ball beautifully and Bernhard Langer shot a 66, while Brown never scowled at Lyle once as the latter got round in 68. They even defeated Ballesteros and Olazabal.

Jacklin's press conference was an amicable affair. All the journalists were genuinely pleased to see him. One or two had caught up with him in the States during the summer, not just to talk about the Ryder Cup but also with regard to his successes on the US Senior tour.

There had been the usual profiles in the magazines and through them all was not only the measure of respect one would expect but also the affection that the man commanded. Jacklin was an interviewer's dream. He was honest and forthright and spoke with an omnipresent sense of passion. In *Golf World* he was asked about the Ryder Cup and he said: 'I can trace my career through it. I have experienced the whole range of emotions that match play golf can produce. It has taken me to cloud nine and dumped me in the gutter. I have beaten Jack Nicklaus in the morning and then halved with him in the afternoon. I have lost two singles matches in one day and both on the last hole. I have captained a Ryder Cup team that has lost by one point and one that has retained the trophy in a halved match. Golf is at its best when it is like this. You see characters change. You see men grow seven feet tall and you see others afraid of what they might find out about themselves.

'A captain sees all this and a captain can bring about these changes. You have to be strong. You have to be autocratic at times and not give in to some of the stronger wills. I remember Ballesteros coming to me once and telling me he wanted to sit out a series of fourballs. I told him he was playing. I didn't say I would like him to play because that would have given him the chance to come back. This is what you have to do sometimes.

'And when you see the light in your players' eyes at the end and you've won the trophy you know it is worth it. You know that all the angst has been worth it and the players know that it was worth it too. That's why they try so hard all year to qualify again, to be at St Andrews for the greatest of all showdowns.'

Jacklin was almost in tears at the end of that interview, an emotional man recalling some emotional times.

And here in the media tent, a more formal gathering maybe, he remained relaxed and ready to impress his charismatic personality on his audience.

An American journalist wanted to know about his two selections: hadn't they caused some controversy? 'Yes, you could say that,' Jacklin said, with a wry smile that was shared by most of his audience. 'I had two desperately difficult choices to make. I had to choose between Ian Woosnam and Dai Rees and time may well prove that I made the wrong decision, I don't know. But I think Woosie at his bulldog best can take on anyone and that's what I'm banking on this week. I believe the fact that some people think I have made the wrong decision will also have a positive effect on Ian and I think we saw a little of that in his German Open victory.

'If choosing between two Welshmen was difficult then choosing between two Scotsmen was no easier! I think Colin Montgomerie will go on to play in a lot of Ryder Cups but I just felt for this occasion that Eric Brown was the right choice. I rang Colin to explain and he wasn't happy, which is what you would hope for in a way. But Eric has an indomitable will and doesn't care who he plays, and his Ryder Cup singles record is unbelievable, really. But if people say I got it wrong then I find it hard to argue. In the end it came down to personal choices and I've stuck my neck on the block with mine.'

Was he happy to hear about the apparent discord in the American camp? Jacklin feigned surprise. 'Really? That's very upsetting, isn't it?', he teased. 'I think I'd be a little restless too if I was up against our guys!'

What did he think of the Old Course? 'It's in fabulous condition. The decision to protect the fairways in the winter by having everyone play off Astroturf has made a hell of a difference. It's better than I've ever seen it before.'

How were his team playing? 'They did all right today. I wouldn't go any stronger than that. Barnesy is usually having a few drinks on a Tuesday lunchtime so it was hard for him to get wound up. Nick knows the place backwards and so he felt it would be better to work with David Leadbetter on the practice ground. Henry Cotton is striking the ball magnificently. Sandy Lyle and Eric Brown defeated Seve and Ollie so that can only be a good sign. Yes, I'm happy. We've got another two days to get everyone attuned but at this stage I'm contented.'

Was this the strongest American team ever? 'I think it would be very hard to argue against that statement. This really is a golden age for American golf. But we've seen it before where even the most gifted players at stroke play struggle in the Ryder Cup and we have a number of things going for us. I think home advantage could prove very important.'

Any clues as to pairings? 'I think you can work out most of them, can't you? You can safely say that Seve and Ollie and Barnesy and Bernard and Nick and Oosty will be partners. I'm certainly happy to reveal that much to you. How the players went out today gives a clue to how I'm thinking but it depends to some extent on form. Obviously I have pairings ideas in my head but if two players are in form and two are not then it is clearly desirable to go with the former whether they have an established partner-ship or not rather than with one of them and his partner who is struggling a wee bit.'

Perhaps aware that they needed to save some questions for later in the week, the journalists ran out of steam. Jacklin was thanked for his attendance and left to a stream of good luck wishes.

On the practice ground, Faldo was still hitting balls. Leadbetter was working on his pupil's posture. 'Why did God have to make me so tall?', Faldo was saying frustratedly. A gorgeous evening was settling upon St Andrews. The waters appeared still in the bay. The corporate side of things was winding down for the afternoon and preparing itself for a few drinks later on. The stand behind the 18th green lay silent but for students earning extra cash by collecting the day's rubbish.

Behind Faldo, though, a goodly crowd was enjoying a bit of overtime viewing. Nor was the Open champion alone there. Twenty yards away, Hogan was hitting drives that never moved from the straight and narrow. Ballesteros was concentrating on some wedge shots with his coach, the eccentric American Mac O'Grady, who had to be feeling a conflict of loyalties. Kite was still there too, and so were Nelson and Sarazen. This time Nelson was not watching Watson but concentrating on his own game. After about twenty shots he would dig into his pocket and bring out a notebook, into which he would scribble some words and etchings. Sarazen just carried on hitting the ball flat out. Six people on the practice ground who kept themselves to themselves and kept the gallery enthralled.

Inside the Old Course Hotel the spa was full of players' wives, who were relaxing after a day's shopping and sightseeing in Edinburgh. Vicki Langer was lifting some weights, and several hotel punters mistook her for one of the opposition as she took breaks occasionally to chat with Linda Watson – two Americans enjoying each other's company.

It had been quite a day. The wives had been picked up at 9 a.m. in a coach, transported to the centre of Edinburgh, and taken round the familiar tourist routes, before being let loose on Princes Street. Many feminists might have frowned at this clichéd scene but these women were enjoying the wealth that their husbands' prowess had brought. For three hours they had prowled the department stores of the Scottish capital and between them they ran up bills amounting to many thousands of pounds. The most extravagant was Trevino's young wife, Claudia, who was visiting Edinburgh for the first time. She was captivated, and spent the sort of sum that it would take most men several months to earn, but not of course her husband, who was enjoying a fine season. It was the sort of sum Trevino would make simply on the strength of one holed putt.

The wives enjoyed mingling too. By necessity, the men were kept apart as befits two teams in combat. But their wives were free in one of the world's great cities and the laughter that accompanied them as they walked and shopped and ate and drank indicated their appreciation at the trip, which had been instigated by Astrid Jacklin.

Several of them slept soundly on the coach back to St Andrews. Arnold Palmer's wife, Winnie, was not among them. A bundle of energy, she looked out of the window as they crossed the Forth Road Bridge before striking up a conversation with Barbara Nicklaus. For all their husbands' rivalry, the two women found it hard not to get along. They knew what the problem was: their partners were two chips off the same block. The wives believed that in time Nicklaus and Palmer would come to appreciate each other's achievements and each other's standing in the game and maybe even a friendship would develop.

'This is one place in the world that you never get sick of visiting, isn't it?', Winnie said.

'There's just such a variety of things to do,' agreed Barbara. 'Jack's never happier than when he is here. Winning the Open at St Andrews was one of the greatest things that ever happened to him.'

For a second Barbara Nicklaus wondered whether she had said

the wrong thing, given that Palmer had never been successful at the Home of Golf. Winnie Palmer read her mind. She needn't have worried. 'Yes, they truly love Jack here, don't they?', Mrs Palmer said.

Astrid Jacklin was delighted at the success of the trip. She was sitting at the front of the coach with Lesley Gallacher and the pair were working on the itinerary for the rest of the week. Tomorrow there would be a stroll through the streets of St Andrews and on Thursday a trip to Loch Lomond.

On Wednesday evening there was the Gala Ball, the highlight of the week's social calendar. On Thursday night both captains had elected to have team dinners with their wives. But before all that there was tonight and a private dinner to be hosted by the Royal and Ancient Golf Club of St Andrews.

———

Lounge suits and cocktail dresses were the required attire for this dinner, which was held in the dining room of the R&A clubhouse. It was a private and splendidly low-key affair. The room held seventy-two people comfortably and that was exactly the number in attendance. In charge of formal proceedings was Michael Bonallack, the R&A's avuncular secretary, who gave the first of the two speeches that were made. He spoke of the club's immense pride at hosting such a dinner. Bonallack, a considerable player himself of course, proved the perfect host. His words skilfully conveyed the importance of the occasion yet didn't embarrass the players by going on too much about their achievements. He told a joke about Trevino, a player whose company he had long enjoyed. Their friendship extended back to the days when they were paired together in the Open at Birkdale. Bonallack told of how in the first round, as they had been waiting to tee off, an ambulance with sirens blazing could clearly be heard. Trevino fell to the ground clutching his chest. The crowd appreciated his black humour and the gesture had relaxed Bonallack as well. All these years on, Trevino, naturally, was still game for a little banter. 'Swingin' any better these days, Michael?', he mischievously asked.

The R&A's clubhouse is one of the best in the world and one of the most spectacular buildings in Scotland. It is perhaps surprising that for the first hundred years of its existence the club did without a home at all, but they more than made up for lost time after consulting, in 1853, the local architect, George Rae.

It may be the most recognizable symbol in golf with its prime location behind the opening tee and the 18th green a short distance to the left. Its rooms are steeped in tradition and grandeur, and are filled with artefacts tracing the club's history. The famous clock that fronts the top of what might be termed the West Wing had just turned 9 p.m. when Bonallack sat down to be congratulated by the captain of the club, who was sitting on his left.

The room was once more filled with conversation. Faldo, who had almost eaten the R&A out of house and home, was having what might, if the assembled company hadn't known the pair well, have been construed as an argument with Sarazen. Sarazen was on to one of his pet subjects, which was the pace of play. The veteran campaigner said: 'It's never easy to come to the end of a playing career, Nick, but I'm glad in some ways to be getting out of it. I don't know how some of you guys take so long. I was behind you at the US PGA and I would have played my iron shot and been up by the green in the amount of time it took you to play your stroke.'

Faldo was unruffled. He had been chided by Sarazen before about his deliberate approach. 'Gene, do I really have to explain this to you again? I just have to feel that everything is right, that my setup is right, that my concentration is right, before I play a shot, and sometimes that takes time. The last thing on my mind is to upset other players and I try to make up for any slowness by walking fast between shots.'

'You upset me,' Sarazen said.

Faldo, who could be amusing company in this sort of gathering, lightened the mood. 'Not as much as I'll upset you when I whup you if we meet this weekend.'

Sarazen, who hadn't meant any real offence anyway, took the bait: 'You'll need more than Oosty to save you this time.'

Brown, who was sitting next to Faldo, enjoyed this last bit. He was in his element when arguing with the Americans. If he had been a cricketer he would have been a prime exponent of that charmless art the Australians refer to as sledging. Now he joined in. As ever, he went further than Faldo. The Englishman was often considered tactless, once having prompted David Feherty to say: 'The only time he opens his mouth is to change feet.'

But Faldo was a positive ambassador in comparison to Brown. 'Twenty years ago, Gene, it might have been a contest. But let's face it, you're past your best and Faldo's at his prime. It wouldn't be a contest.' Brown meant it as a joke. Sarazen felt like thumping him in the face. Thankfully he did not. All around them the conversation had stopped, as is often the case when someone is saying something particularly interesting. A waiter broke the ice by offering some more wine and Brown accepted readily. Not many players did, however. Most were trying to stay as close as possible to their normal routines and if it was Tuesday night then there was only one full day to go before the start of the tournament. The most popular drink, by far, was Highland Spring water.

Hagen was having water too but just a splash and on top of some Scotch. As ever, drinking was not compromising his alertness. He saw the Brown–Sarazen situation out of the corner of his eye, and as the embarrassed silence fell between them for a moment, he considered this was the time to rise from his chair and formally thank the R&A for the evening. In truth the occasion was such that a speech wasn't necessary but Hagen was never slow to proffer words of gratitude when he had enjoyed himself. 'I have no doubt that this will be the greatest Ryder Cup of all and the fact that it is to be staged here at St Andrews is part of the reason,' he said. 'What promises to be a special week has got off to a very special start tonight and on behalf of both teams I'd like to thank the R&A for an evening that will form part of our memories of a great occasion.'

Hagen, as ever, couldn't resist a ribald postscript. 'You'll have noted, gentlemen, how certain players have extended the hand of bonhomie to one another already,' he said, to general laughter. Hagen looked at Sarazen and then Brown. Sarazen caught the spirit of his captain's words and smiled.

Brown just looked back at him with a face cast in granite. He mouthed three words at Hagen, slowly so there could be no way Hagen could not understand. 'Fancy bloody dan,' he said.

As the formal proceedings broke up, all parties retired to the library for one last drink or a coffee. It was still only 9.15 p.m. The guests settled back into snug leather armchairs or sofas and many admired the priceless paintings that adorned all four walls.

They had now broken up into clusters, each comprising the sort of people with whom they would normally spend this part of the evening if they were all on tour. The Faldos were happily rabbiting away with the Gallachers, for example. The Woosnams were conversing with the O'Connors.

Snead was bitching. 'I hate these type of occasions,' he said to Trevino, who fully shared his sentiments. 'What has all this to do with the Ryder Cup? Everything should be taken care of so that all we have to do is play golf and practise, and our leisure time should be our own. We shouldn't have to do this. I'm going in a minute if Hagen hasn't taken care of business.'

Hagen had, or rather the organizers had. The cars that would ferry the teams back to the hotel would leave in fifteen minutes – which left Hogan and Bonallack plenty of time to continue their animated conversation about Carnoustie.

Bonallack had wandered up to Hogan to enquire about his morning's experience of the great links and had been surprised at the warmth and the depth of the American's conversation. They discussed each hole in detail: its strengths and weaknesses; the correct line; the right strategy. Bonallack was telling Hogan of the time when Carnoustie staged two Amateur Championships in the space of seven years when Bonallack had been in his prime. Indeed, during that time he had won the title on no fewer than four occasions but, to his considerable chagrin, none had been over the championship course at Carnoustie.

Hogan, who usually detested these occasions as much as Snead, was enjoying this interlude. He then made a familiar American offer but one that shocked Bonallack because he knew that coming from this particular American it meant something. 'If you're in my neighbourhood sometime you must stop by and stay a few days,' Hogan said. Bonallack was delighted and felt like getting his diary out there and then.

Snead was the first into the chauffeured cars. It was now 10 p.m. and the night air was cool. A couple of photographers gathered around the entrance to the clubhouse as the last farewells were said.

The lights were on in St Andrews. In The Niblick, at the corner of Golf Place, the numbers who wanted to drink far outweighed the space available and they spilled out on to the street. In the restaurant upstairs the diners chose from a themed menu with items such as Hagen steak (full of flavour) or Jacklin pie (a real crowd pleaser). All over the town the bars were full and the eateries remained packed even at this late hour, and in every establishment the conversation was invariably focused on golf. On the pavement outside The Niblick, a couple of right golfing bores were arguing about Jacklin's decision to go with Brown instead of Montgomerie, one taking either side. Inevitably others joined in and as Jacklin made his way out of the clubhouse it had become so loud that even the man himself may have caught the gist of it all. If he did, he betrayed no emotion, but the two men noticed Jacklin as the car went by and they laughed to themselves and invited him for a drink and a discussion. Jacklin merely saw their gesticulations. He waved and smiled. The car drove on.

Back at the hotel, Hagen was ready for some more to drink. Jacklin declined his invitation. He had also instructed his team to either go to their rooms or to the Jacklin Room upon their return.

Hagen was not afraid to go to the packed public bar in the hotel. A few people duly started tapping the shoulders of their drinking companions and pointing in his direction. Hagen looked around him and thought about staying for a moment and catching the general breeze of conversation. While he weighed up his options a middle-aged woman duly approached and asked him for his autograph. She was American and had a story to tell. 'I'm afraid I'm not a fan of golf,' she said. 'It was my husband's idea to come. We flew on Concorde but I didn't get a chance to ask you for your autograph then. I'm a great fan of your films.'

Hagen smiled. 'Where's your husband?', he asked.

'Why, he's over there. Would you like to meet him and have a drink?', she said, not dreaming for a moment that the man in front of her would accept her invitation.

Hagen smiled again. 'Why, I don't mind if I do,' he said. The woman almost fainted. She was having a conversation with a film star!

Hagen didn't stay long. This wasn't because he found them boring or uncommunicative. Far from it. Hagen was relaxed in everyone's company. But over on the far side of the room he saw a party of officials from the PGA of America and felt duty-bound at least to say hello. He was greeted warmly by the organization's president. He had been at the R&A dinner too but protocol had demanded that he and Hagen be kept apart on the top table. In fact the pair hadn't spoke since the trip over on Concorde. Hagen asked the president what he had done during the day and was told that he had played the course that Peter Thomson had designed some years earlier on the outskirts of town. In turn the official wanted to know about that day's practice. 'Went like a dream,' Hagen said. 'Tonight was even better. Eric Brown insulted Gene and he's as mad as hell. You know he plays his best golf in that state. Sam's getting nicely wound up as well, and Jack is going to be an absolute star. Ben had a terrific time at Carnoustie. It's done him the world of good. I just couldn't be happier. Indeed I'm so happy I'm going to let you buy me another Scotch with a dash of that Highland water stuff.'

It would be past midnight before Hagen and the PGA of America officials left the bar. They were far from the last to leave. There was a lovely atmosphere in the room, as so often happens when people have had just a little too much to drink. New friendships were being made as spectators in town for the week met others with whom they had so much in common. All around, the same phrase was being repeated, over and over again: 'Oh, go on, let's have one more for the road.' Indeed, similar words were being said in bars throughout St Andrews. It was Tuesday night and the contest was edging ever closer and the excitement was building. It had got to the stage where those who were coming for the golf had now arrived and were determined to enjoy themselves. At The Niblick the two bores had stopped talking about Brown and Montgomerie and had moved on to Hagen's two selections. Again they had differing opinions, and this time they had been joined by half a dozen Americans, who all had views of their own.

It was all good-natured. Brown was now good-natured as well, as he retired to bed after a couple of drinks with Barnes and O'Connor. Snead was no longer irascible. Sarazen was vowing to beat the living daylights (metaphorically, of course) out of Brown, not to mention Faldo. Cotton's stomach was playing up. Faldo had thought about ringing room service but had dropped off to sleep instead, with some words of wisdom from Leadbetter lodged in his brain.

Jacklin slept soundly as well. And eventually the town would too. The twenty-four players, meanwhile, would be up and ready to practise once more just a couple of hours after the last reveller had downed his last drink and tried to remember where the hell he was supposed to rest his head for what remained of the night.

3

Wednesday:
A Gala Occasion

ST ANDREWS IS never better than on those days in late September when autumn is preparing to unfold. The town, and certainly the golf course, may lack avenues of trees with leaves of every conceivable shade of brown. But it possesses a stark beauty that more than compensates, and the town's mix of students who have returned from their vacation and golfers desperate for one last whiff of the summer wine is indeed an intoxicating one.

It is entirely appropriate for a place where golf made its home that its streets are compact and the best way to see the intriguing array of historical sites and monuments is by walking. And this is what Tom and Linda Watson did, forty-eight hours before the first shots in the Ryder Cup were to be played.

Having ordered breakfast in their room they began early, just as the sun came up on St Andrews Bay on what would prove a beautiful and spectacularly picturesque day. Out of the hotel they strode past the fated 17th that had once caused Watson such pain. The hole looked beautiful, stretching back in the direction of the rising sun. Arm in arm, they walked along The Links road, past the Russacks Hotel where others who liked these early hours could be seen peering from the lounge windows.

As they passed the 18th green Watson could not resist standing and lingering for a second, wondering what it had in store for him this week. At the junction with Golf Place they turned left and then sharply right into The Scores, and past the hotel of that name and the Sea Life centre on the left. On their right were scores of buildings given over to learning, among them the history and the biology faculties. In a couple of short hours these rooms would be full of students for whom the worries and concerns of what happened to two teams over the Old Course would, at least for a while, be of little concern.

Towards the end of The Scores (which, incidentally, did not take its name from golf but comes in fact from a Norse word meaning cliff top) they paused at St Andrews Castle. Watson had been meaning to look around the remains of this medieval structure for some years now but had never got round to it. He wouldn't this week either, for at that early hour it was closed. Nevertheless, from the street it was possible to appreciate its dramatic location on the bay, and against the blue sky the ruins looked proud and desolate. In the middle of the street, Linda Watson spotted something and at first thought it was the initials T.W. 'Anything to do with you?', she said, smiling. The first letter in fact was a G and referred to the Protestant reformer, George Wishart, who was burned on that spot, having the previous day been tried in the cathedral and found guilty of heresy.

The cathedral itself was just a few yards further on. Owing to the volatile nature of medieval Scotland it took a hundred and fifty years to complete and then was left to crumble and decay for a further three hundred years as the locals, whipped into a frenzy by the sermons of the fiery Protestant preacher John Knox, used it as a quarry and built houses with its stones. Even so, the ruins that are left form an indispensable part of the fabric and the charm of the town. Watson loved to wander among the gravestones in the cathedral and he knew that his wife would find it interesting too. Inevitably they stumbled across the memorials to Young Tom and Old Tom Morris, who between them won eight of the first twelve Opens held. Young Tom won it three years in a row and was awarded outright the belt that was given to the winner. It was replaced by the auld claret jug that remains the prize today and it was appropriate that Young Tom won that too in the first year for which it was played.

Of course, the competition was nothing like the present, but then Young Tom's career was savagely cut short like no other, since he died at the age of just 24 of what was said to be a broken heart. Linda Watson read the moving words that grace the memorial:

Deeply regretted by numerous friends and all golfers,
He thrice in succession won the champion's belt;
And held it without rivalry and yet without envy;
His many amiable qualities
Being no less acknowledged than his golfing achievements.

Having passed through the cemetery the Watsons gazed upon the tall belltower of St Rule's Church. St Rule was a Greek monk who is reputed to have brought the bones of St Andrew to Fife under the guidance of an angel. When he arrived at St Andrews, Rule was saved from almost certain death at the hands of Angus, the King of the Picts, by the appearance of a huge white cross, or saltire, that dominated the blue sky. Thus did Scotland gain its patron saint and its national emblem, which now flew proudly from the masts by the R&A clubhouse, as did the flags of every other nation that boasted a Ryder Cup representative.

Tom Watson figured they had time, before heading back, to see St Mary's on the Rock, which is where the history of St Andrews began in the year 700. They had been out for almost two hours and at the Old Course Hotel the rest of the American team were finishing their breakfasts and preparing to go out on to the links.

———

The Europeans were already on the practice ground. It was their turn to be first on to the tee. They could hardly wait. It was just 8.45 a.m. and it had already turned into one of those days when it was just a joy to hold a golf club in one's hands; it didn't matter how good the golfer or how often the person played, the feeling always remained.

Ballesteros was radiant. It had been a good year for the Spaniard. The problems with his back had, for the moment anyway, receded, and now as golfing middle age approached he had acquired a maturity that had allowed him to accept that playing well all the time was impossible but that he could still enjoy his share of good days. The smile on his face indicated that he expected to have a good week. He wrapped a fatherly arm around Olazabal, who let go of the poker-faced expression on show during his practising as the pair shared a few gentle remarks.

As they made their way towards the first tee Brown was even talking to Lyle, which came as quite a pleasant bonus to the latter.

So little had they spoken on the previous day that Lyle was thinking of wearing a Walkman between shots. 'Same as yesterday, Sandy,' Brown said. 'No mercy. I need that money.'

'Well,' Sandy mused, 'it was better than saying nothing.'

A rousing cheer greeted the two Scots as they made their way on to the first tee. Their opponents today would be Cotton and Langer, an obdurate duo if ever there was one.

Like the Americans the previous day, the Europeans played nine holes of foursomes and nine of fourballs. There were a couple of cracking matches. Brown and Lyle confirmed the promise they had shown the previous day. Under Brown's stewardship, Lyle once more played his best foursomes golf. Normally he couldn't play this form of golf to save his life but now it was as if he were doing just that. Brown and Lyle turned 2 up and although Cotton birdied the 10th and 11th, Lyle's power down the long 14th proved crucial as he notched the winning birdie. At the 17th, as Cotton and Langer both aimed for the front of the green, Lyle produced a miraculous second shot to 3 ft. Lyle looked across to Brown and wondered whether he might even say 'Good shot!' What Brown actually said was: 'You great Scottish puddin'. You should have saved that for Friday.' As Lyle turned away and sulked, Brown had a quiet smile to himself. That was twenty-five quid won.

A 2 and 1 victory for Brown and Lyle was followed by a similar victory for Woosnam and O'Connor over Faldo and Oosterhuis. The latter couldn't repeat the ball striking he had shown the day before and Faldo was still bemoaning his posture. He stood in the middle of several fairways playing imaginary shots with his knees bent in an exaggerated pose. Woosnam looked back at him with a rather disgusted look.

Woosnam didn't think much of Faldo. They had once formed a terrific Ryder Cup partnership but now everyone wondered how it had lasted over a whole Ryder Cup. The pair were chalk and cheese on the course and even more different off it. Faldo found it hard to get on with anyone who didn't share his own single-mindedness. As there were only a handful of such dedicated people on the whole planet at any one time it meant his close friends were not exactly numerous.

The Welshman offered a total contrast. Woosnam had come into the game for what he could get out of it, whereas Faldo had always been in it for the glory. Woosnam's aims might have changed over the years, the need for a buck having rather receded as his bank account rose above several millions, but he still found it hard to discover what made Faldo tick.

He wasn't much worried about those sorts of things now, however. His win on Sunday had given him confidence and now he could feel that he was about to put together a succession of good results. It was an important time of year. After the Ryder Cup there was still the World Match Play to go for, and Woosnam relished these tournaments, which varied the staple diet of stroke play. He also had something to prove. He hadn't enjoyed the newspaper headlines that had suggested that Rees would have been a much better choice in the team than himself. Ballesteros had come up to him and said: 'All my life, Ian, I have been at my best when I want to prove people wrong and I reckon that applies to you this week.' Woosnam had those words at the forefront of his mind.

The crowds, though, had gathered to watch Spain v. Scotland and it was an indication of his enduring popularity that the locals found it very hard to cheer against Ballesteros even if he was partnering Olazabal against Barnes and Gallacher. It was the Scots who came out on top, though. Just to be contrary, this quartet played foursomes over the back nine, because Ballesteros wanted to play the 17th in this format. Perhaps he was wishing afterwards that he had not made such a request. It was his drive that sailed out of bounds to put the home pair 1 ahead playing the last.

Ballesteros tried to make amends with a gorgeous approach that finished adjacent to the flag but Gallacher sank a 12-ft putt down the final green for a matching birdie. So once more the Spaniards had lost in practice and as they came off the 18th green, the watching Jacklin rather liked the chilly look in Ballesteros's eye, which seemed to say: 'This is practice. It won't happen when we're under the gun.'

———————

A lunch of soup and sandwiches, and the European team were led into the media room. They dominated the small platform. Few of them looked as if they were about to enjoy the next hour or so.

Faldo, in particular, sat hunched, his head resting in his right palm.

Jacklin opened the proceedings. He was asked a few gentle questions about the previous night's dinner and of course he made no mention of the little contretemps between Brown and Sarazen. He was asked about his team's form and he answered truthfully that the standard of golf had been a great deal better than the previous day. 'I'm delighted that Seve and Ollie have lost again,' he said. 'I'll be absolutely ecstatic if they lose again tomorrow because I know there is just no way in hell that they could lose four times in a row come Friday.'

Jacklin praised the attitude of his team. 'It's hard for these guys who play week in, week out to fall into what is really a totally different routine but they have done so with total professionalism. We are all getting along famously. My main worry is who to leave out in the Friday foursomes. Normally I can rely on at least leaving Sandy out because that's not his game but he played out of his skin with Eric today.'

After Jacklin's opening remarks, each player was given the opportunity to describe what the week meant to him and what he was hoping it would bring.

Woosnam: Obviously the most important thing is that we win the trophy. We haven't won it for . . . how long is it now? Six years? Six years. Well, it's a pride thing now. We need to win it back.

Cotton: I think there are several players in this team that do not enjoy losing to the Yanks in particular and I think that is the key to how this Ryder Cup is going to go.

Faldo: I'm looking forward to it. I'm not playing very well in practice but it's nearly there. This place usually brings out something special in me.

Lyle: We've got home advantage and that is a big plus. We could do with the weather turning a bit cold and a bit nasty. I think that would suit us down to the ground.

Ballesteros: I think it is fantastic to be playing the Ryder Cup at the Home of Golf and we have a fantastic team, and a great chance of winning.

Olazabal: We're all going to have to play at the very peak of our form to stand a chance of winning. The American team is very strong but I am very confident we can do it.

Oosterhuis: We've got to concentrate on our own games and not worry about the opposition. We've got to do our very best and if that doesn't prove good enough then so be it.

Gallacher: As Seve said, the Americans are very strong but so are we and St Andrews gives us a great opportunity to win. The home crowd will be a big factor and they could prove very inspirational.

Barnes: I think we've got too many reliable partnerships to lose. I think we'll be very strong in the fourballs and foursomes.

O'Connor: It's a great privilege to be in this team and I am very confident that we will do very well. It's going to be a very close match and in the end may come down to a point either way but I think we'll do it.

Langer: I agree with most of my team-mates. They are very strong but so are we and home advantage could well prove decisive.

Brown: We've nothing to fear. St Andrews will scare the living daylights out of the Americans. If we go out there and do the business then there is no way that we will not win.

It was left to Jacklin to add a postscript: 'As you can see, ladies and gentleman, Eric is his normal worried self.'

The questions began. The usual things first. Players were asked about their form. Jacklin was asked whether events were going as he planned. He was then asked about the envelope system, in which the name of a player is put in a sealed envelope the night before the singles matches, to be paired off with any member of the opposition who is declared unfit to play. Jacklin described it as an unfortunate system but he could not think of a better one. He had rejected the notion of a travelling reserve, an idea put forward by Hagen. 'I don't think it is possible for a reserve to prepare mentally. It is unfair on the player, even more unfair than the envelope system in my view,' Jacklin said.

A journalist from the Spanish newspaper *El País* asked him to talk about the Ballesteros–Olazabal partnership. It was a question that Jacklin had been asked hundreds of times but as ever he gave it thought and responded courteously. 'I think you all know my feelings about Seve. He is, for me, the most naturally talented player that I have ever seen. He plays shots of which others are not capable, and this contest brings out the best in him. The record books show that Ballesteros has won nothing like the majors of, say, a Nicklaus but some of his performances in the Ryder Cup have been superhuman. You should see him come Sunday night. He can hardly support his own weight, he's given so much of himself.

'When he first played with José Maria he carried him but now there are occasions when it is the other way around. They are the best Ryder Cup partnership that I have come across and without them I wouldn't fancy our chances this week quite as much as I do.'

After the perfunctory opening questions, press conferences often evolved like this. The Spanish journalists wanted to know about the Spaniards. The Irish wanted Jacklin to talk about O'Connor, or for the great man to speak for himself. Those representing the tabloids wanted quotes from Faldo. They were next.

Would he relish a head-to-head against Nicklaus? one wanted to know of Faldo. Would victory in such a match prove something to himself? 'Yeah, I'd love to go up against Jack,' Faldo said. 'He was the reason I got into golf in the first place. He's the greatest player of all. Sure I'd get a buzz out of beating him but it wouldn't prove anything. He's got eighteen major championship victories and I haven't. Beating him head to head wouldn't prove anything on that score. Anything can happen on the day.'

Jacklin was asked if he'd had any pleasant surprises so far during the week, and he said that he was very pleased with the good luck charm that Astrid had bought him in Edinburgh. 'Seriously,' he said, 'I like the look of Sandy. He looks bang on his game and we all know how good he is in those circumstances.'

The journalist from *El País* again: with a broad grin he asked Seve whether he'd ever lost three matches in a row before. Ballesteros feigned his incomprehension, as he had on hundreds of occasions in the past. It was his way of giving himself a couple of seconds to come up with a witty response. 'You say I'm no good any more?', he said playfully. The questioner looked a touch embarrassed. 'Would you like to take me on?' Everyone had seen this act of Ballesteros but no one minded seeing it again. It was indicative of the warmth that existed between him and the press. There were a couple of players on the top platform who didn't mind talking with certain sections of the media while most didn't like it at all. But only Ballesteros, Jacklin and Cotton would talk freely, without reservation, to any pressman and it was hardly a coincidence that a mutual bond of respect had developed between those three players and the representatives who sat before them. 'I may well have lost three matches in practice before,' Ballesteros eventually answered. 'I don't like to get Tony's hopes up too high and I like to surprise the opposition by playing well on Friday morning. I'm fine. I'm not hitting it great but there's two days to go. That's a long time in golf.'

Cotton, the oldest member of the European team, was asked for a few comments. He looked as immaculate as ever. His black trousers possessed a knife-edge crease. His white shirt showed off his still firm physique. There was not a hair out of place on his head. With his dress sense and his swarthy complexion, Cotton looked every inch the Latin lover. It was hardly any wonder, then, that clothing sponsors had queued up for him to model their products. This wasn't an act on Cotton's part to attract their money. This was how he was, and when he spoke he had the coolly arrogant air of one who knew that people hung on his words. 'Gentlemen, I hope you'll excuse me in a second because I have an appointment with my Belgian masseur, who's keeping me supple and pliable and in condition to take on these Yankee upstarts. Yes, I think it will be a grand match, and I hope the crowd are suitably biased and give us the support that will swing the match in our favour. The last thing we want is to lose the match again, although I don't want you tabloid chaps to run off with the wrong idea. When I say biased I don't mean booing the opposition. But I want them to make known which team they want to win. I want to stand on the 9th tee and hear a cheer from the 3rd and know instantly by the volume whether it's a cheer for us or the opposition.' And with that Cotton left the platform for his date with his masseur, who, with his waxed moustache and roly-poly shape, could have doubled for another famous Belgian, Hercule Poirot.

The conference was breaking up anyway. Not that the other players could escape as easily as had Cotton. Most of them were cornered by clusters of journalists, anxious for more quotes. Jacklin was escorted to the BBC radio box.

———————————

The American press conference was not due to start for another half-hour, and several writers wondered what sort of mood Hagen would be in. It was certainly to their benefit that the meeting had not been scheduled at breakfast time because the American captain had been in a foul mood. For a start he had woken with a hangover. But that was easing when he began to look through the selection of newspapers that had been pushed under his door. 'Yanks in Turmoil', read one headline. 'Jacked Off' was another, complete with a strap headline: 'Arnie and Nicklaus in Ryder Rumpus'. The most favourable he could find was 'Yankee Doddle', a story referring to his comments about the overwhelming likelihood of an American victory.

Hagen was never one to dwell on a bad press, though. Privately, he was almost ready to laugh them off as he met his team in the Hagen Room. But he promised himself that he would have one or two jokes at the expense of certain writers that afternoon.

There were no games today from Hagen. He sent his men out in the formations from which he would hope to choose come Friday morning. Kite and Lema took the money this time. For Lema, playing in the Ryder Cup at St Andrews was an unbridled thrill. His Open victory there had come despite his having had just one practice round. He had borrowed Palmer's caddie, Tip Anderson, and said later that he had just hit the ball wherever he had been told. This was written up as false modesty but in fact there was a great deal of truth in it. Of course, hitting the ball where one is told is not an insignificant skill in itself but Lema really did follow all the lines advocated by Anderson and similarly, on the greens, he allowed him to read all the putts.

His great achievement had come on the final day when two rounds were played. Lema began poorly and by the time he got to the 6th hole, which shares its green with the 12th, he instinctively felt that the lead he held was slipping away. He casually sauntered over to Nicklaus, who was playing the latter hole. Lema's instincts were correct. His 9-shot advantage over the Golden Bear had ebbed away to 1. Yet he didn't panic or become daunted. He played the next five holes in 15 shots on his way to a 68. A final round of 70 saw him home by 5 strokes.

Lema enjoyed the rapport he had with the St Andrews people. They liked the way he had shifted much of the praise for his Open victory on to the shoulders of one of their own, namely Anderson. They appreciated his stylish swing and relaxed manner, and the way he enjoyed the enormous wealth that his golfing successes had brought him. Kite and Lema had gone around in 63 but the latter was not about to get carried away. He joshed with some spectators on the 16th tee, when someone had complimented him on his scoring. 'Not the real St Andrews today is it?', he said. 'Could do with a little breeze.'

Snead was upset with Mangrum, who had missed a 10-ft putt on the final green. They had gone round in 64 and not only did they lose the overall stake but they lost their individual match as well, since they were playing Kite and Lema. 'This ain't a good start to the week, Lloyd,' Snead said. 'Damned golf course. Why don't they do something with it? Why don't they come over to America and see all the improvements we have made to our golf courses and copy some of them?'

At least the weather was more to Snead's liking. He hated the cold and he hated having to wear waterproofs. But even he had needed no more than one sweater over his polo neck. Not that this was much consolation now, not when he had just lost another fifty bucks.

Of course Lema made him feel worse too. Snead didn't like losing to Lema, not to a man who seemed so relaxed and ebullient and yet clearly had some steel somewhere deep inside. Snead would much rather lose to someone whose determination showed in the lines in his face. Someone like Eric Brown.

Once more, Hagen had seen little to concern him with regard to his players' form. On this day, when just the merest zephyr disturbed the flags, all of his team had broken par and only Trevino and Casper had failed to break 70.

Casper had been characteristically quiet all week. He was just getting on with the job. He had brought with him his yardage books from previous St Andrews Opens and now was just familiarizing himself with his strategy. The diagrams showed how far he should hit each drive and to where; what part of the greens he should aim for with his second shots; where the real danger lay on each hole and how to avoid it.

The only real conversation he had had with Hagen over the last couple of days was to complain about the uniforms, which he thought were far too bright and gaudy. 'Why can't we play in blue, or grey, or black?', he wanted to know.

'Lighten up, Billy,' Hagen had replied, before collapsing in hysterics at the unintended pun.

A sort of embarrassed silence fell on the media room as Hagen entered. Hagen wore a sombre expression although his earlier feelings of rage had long dissipated. Of course, he wasn't going to let the assembled company know that. Not at the start anyway.

The American team filed into the room a couple of minutes later. Nicklaus and Palmer made a point of talking to one another and laughing and smiling as they came into view. It was a convincing act. Trevino shook hands with a journalist he had known for a long time, who was sitting near the door on the front row. Palmer nodded his acknowledgement to a long-serving columnist from the *Los Angeles Times*.

Hagen set the ball rolling. 'We're in total disarray,' he said. 'As you can, see, gentlemen, Jack and Arnie can't stand the sight of one another and it's clearly having a terrible effect on Jack's golf. He needed a full driver to reach the front of the 18th green today. Tom Kite and Tony Lema couldn't muster anything better than a 63, so they'll have to be taken out of consideration from playing, and Sam is as mad as hell partly because he lost his money again but mostly because he and Lloyd only went round in 64.

'Tom Watson went for a walk around St Andrews this morning and I hope he said a prayer for us when he reached the church at the end of the street. Because clearly, with just two days to go, we're gonna need it.'

It was classic Hagen. He could have been on the silver screen. Several journalists felt like applauding. Many smiled at his cheek. Hagen looked straight into the eyes of one reporter. ' "Ryder Rumpus", Tom,' Hagen said, slowly shaking his head. 'Can't you do any better than that?'

Hagen was in his element now. He had caught everyone on the back foot. It was all going to be plain sailing from now on in. In truth few people minded and certainly none of the regular golf correspondents. Hagen was as popular as Jacklin in these circles.

As with the European team, each of the Americans was invited in turn for a comment on their own golf and the match in prospect.

Nicklaus: We're under no illusions. Any Ryder Cup match in Europe is a tough proposition these days. I've the utmost respect for Tony Jacklin and I know he will have his team believing they can win. We're going to have to play well, it's as simple as that. As to my own game, it's shaping up pretty well. There's one or two things to work on but I'm confident that by Friday I will be ready.'

Palmer: I hope you'll be ready, partner! No seriously, as Jack says, it's going to be a very tough match. The course is in beautiful shape, the best in fact that I've seen it, and we're just going to have to go out and do the damned business if we want to take the cup back.

Watson: I went for a walk around the town today and the history of this place is so awe-inspiring. This is golf as it was meant to be played and I'm just disappointed that my kids are not here to see it all. It's going to be a great match, one of the best Ryder Cups of all time, and at the end of it we're going to win.

Hogan: I've nothing to add to what's already been said.

Lema: I couldn't agree more with Tom's comments. This is a neat place, and I like it even more now than when I won here. Everyone is so friendly. I had conversations with the locals for most of the way round. It seems to me we're all playing well. I played with Tom Kite and Sam and Lloyd today and they all played just great. Sam, you know you haven't given me my winnings yet, don't you? (Snead said nothing.)

Nelson: I can't say I'm too excited with the way I'm playing. My driving needs working on. My chipping is poor. I'm not concentrating properly. I've got a lot of work to do before Friday. The match itself is going to be a close one.

Sarazen: I'm really not interested in what they're doing but how we're playing. Take no notice of Byron. You know what he's like. As the elder statesman of this team I have to say I can't see a weak link. I've not seen a finer side and I will be most surprised if we don't return with the cup.

Trevino: We need some wind. The golf course is not a true test right now. It's too easy. It wasn't meant to be played as it is currently playing. If the weather stays like this then anything can happen. Luck could play a big part, but I hope that doesn't prove the case.

Snead: The golf course is not a true test whatever the wind might do because it just isn't a very good golf course. There are many better places where we could have held this contest. The greens have far too much grain in them. Having said that, I like our chances. Lloyd and I didn't play as well as we could today. We missed a couple of vital putts. But I'll straighten him out by Friday!

Mangrum: The most important thing is for the match to be played in the right spirit and I'm sure that will be the case. We must ensure that golf comes out of this the winner because there will be so many people watching on television who will be influenced by the events that take place. Obviously I hope we win but I feel it will be a great match and a great occasion.

Kite: I agree with Lee in that I think we need a little wind. But it's great playing here. Sam, I can't believe you don't think this is a great place to come and play golf. I'm happy with my own form right now. I'm starting to hole a few putts. I enjoy the Ryder Cup. I like the competition and I like winning.

Hagen said: 'Well put, gentlemen. Are there any questions?'

The American journalists were not convinced by the show for the cameras of Nicklaus and Palmer. One stood up. 'I'd like to ask something of Jack and Arnie. Of course we've known for years that you've had a deadly rivalry and that this has meant that you're not the best of friends. But is this rivalry cooling off now? Are you guys getting any closer to one another?' Palmer said candidly: 'I think we're two very similar people. We're both winners and sure, there are areas of our lives where our paths have conflicted and so it is inevitable that we were not bosom buddies at one stage. But I'm sure I speak for Jack when I say there is absolutely no acrimony between us or anything like that. The story this morning was wrong. I'd be happy to play with Jack and I feel sure he will say the same about partnering me.'

'Absolutely,' said Nicklaus. 'I think Arnold has summed up the situation very well. Everywhere we go we're in competition, whether it is in golf or designing courses or clothing. I think as we are both getting older, as so often happens, our respect for each other has grown. I think we both like the standing that we now have in the game.'

Hagen was proud of his boys. He knew they would play along with the press. He knew also that it wasn't just an act. There had been a thawing of relationships between them. 'Why,' he thought to himself, 'I bet by the time they get to be 50 or 60 they'll be hanging out together and ringing each other up to play in practice rounds and the like.'

Another American journalist took his life in his hands and asked Hogan a question. 'I'd like to ask Ben about Carnoustie,' he said.

For a moment there was no sound. Then Hogan spoke. 'That's a private thing and nothing to do with the Ryder Cup. It doesn't concern anyone,' he said.

The British writers sensed that Snead was their story. 'Why do you hate St Andrews so much?', he was asked.

'What is there to love about it?', he replied.

'What about the tradition?'

'If tradition means poorly prepared golf courses and eggs that are undercooked and warm beer then I'll stick to modern.'

'What about the 17th? Isn't that a great hole?'

'Call the 17th a great hole, huh? You ever played golf? The 17th is a garbage hole. A blind drive and an unfair second shot. It's one of the worst holes I ever played.'

'Sam, do you think the Ryder Cup should always be played in America?'

'No. Don't be silly,' he replied. Snead waited a moment before adding: 'Should always be played in West Virginia.' It was a joke. Possibly.

———

To call it a tent implies some relation to the structure Scouts take with them when they go camping. In fact, such was its size, it was more like a media village than a media tent. It was situated on land adjacent to the clubhouse and so offered wonderful access to the first tee. It was so vast that it stretched the seventy-five or so yards to the road that separates the course from the beach, and then it sprawled, at a right angle, for a further seventy-five yards.

The media people were spoiled rotten in many ways. Some never moved from these quarters all week, except to go back to their hotels or rented houses to sleep. They thought there was no need. Every major newspaper was supplied with a television which beamed the BBC pictures covering every hole. The players were brought to them on one day and the captains every day, and full transcripts of every dot and comma were available within thirty minutes of the end of the interview.

Most of the golf correspondents for the daily papers, though, used these interviews to top up features that they had long had in the word processor. The planning had gone on for some weeks. Some had approached the American players at the US PGA Championship in the middle of August, or, better still, flown out a week earlier or a week later to catch a player in more relaxed surroundings at a less important tournament. Now they were merely monitoring what each golfer was saying, just in case he came out with something extraordinary, or said something they had overlooked.

It's a standing joke that some writers cover the golf circuit from the press tent but in many instances it is the best place to do the job. Go out on to the course to watch a particular player or match and it is a certainty that all the action will be happening elsewhere. The transcripts do not just encourage laziness. If they were not available then no reporter would be able to move from the tent because none of them could afford to miss an interview.

Of course, the Ryder Cup was slightly easier in this respect since, apart from the final day, there was only four matches on the course at any one time. In any case, every newspaper had at least two representatives and so one could always act as cover while another went out to get some 'colour' material by following the golf.

A large restaurant in the media tent supplied food and alcohol to both reporters and photographers from 7 a.m. to 10 p.m. Hot and cold drinks were supplied free of charge. There was also a lounge where the media people could sit, relax, and digest all the words they and their rivals had written.

The sponsors, Johnnie Walker, had set up a hospitality unit next door to the press area where they could have a drink after their work was finished. For the golf correspondents, this was a fairly normal service. For other sports writers, drafted in for the week, it was certainly better than covering a Coca-Cola Cup replay on a cold and wet Wednesday evening.

The American journalists were impressed as well. In many respects the Americans may be the leaders but not when it comes to helping the media do their job. American scoreboards are poor, for a start, and frequently the press are housed some way from where the players would be finishing their rounds. For those operating on British time with deadlines at a premium, it was often a nightmarish experience. The Americans didn't like it much either. So what a wonderful experience it was for them to come to Britain, and find the journalists held in such high esteem!

The Ryder Cup was now almost as big an event in America as it had been in Britain since its inception. Even though the football season had resumed in the States there was hardly a large city newspaper that hadn't sent at least a columnist and usually its golf correspondent as well. What a far cry this was from as recently as a decade ago, when only the *New York Times* and the Associated Press and the two main magazines, *Golf Digest* and *Golf*, had considered it worth the expense. Such was the growth in the popularity of the Ryder Cup, a tournament that once had been seen as America's cup but not now, even after two wins and a tie in the last three matches.

But all this media interest from America was the result of something else as well: they were responding to the extraordinary appeal of this particular American team, and the fact that they were captained by a noted Hollywood actor only broadened that popularity. It was clear that whatever happened in this Ryder Cup, the shots played would certainly be heard around the world.

The American players almost collided with their wives as they came out of the media area. The wives of both teams in fact were winding up their tour of St Andrews following a walk along the deserted beach. The light autumn breeze was sufficient to give their cheeks a ruddy hue and the contemplative stroll much pause for thought. Most were itching to talk. All of them were looking forward to the Gala Ball. Inevitably what to wear had figured highly in the equation. The wives on each side had discussed this in detail among themselves weeks before the event. Now they swapped information.

For Linda Watson, the walk had involved going over some of the ground she had covered earlier in the day with her husband. She was able to explain some of the notable landmarks. She even managed to fit in a walk around the castle, which, she smiled to herself, would cause her husband some chagrin later. She had had her picture taken on the battlements, a profile portrait as she stared pensively out at a sea that was calm and empty save for some seagulls that squawked endlessly as they continued their search for food.

The part had walked along the main streets of the town: Market Street, and North and South Street. Their guide for the day read out some of the words of the revered golf writer, Bernard Darwin, who wrote in the early years of the century: 'It may be immoral, but it is delightful to see a whole town given up to golf;

to see the butcher and the baker and the candlestick maker
shouldering his clubs as soon as his day's work is done and making
a dash for the links.'

In truth, the streets of St Andrews have rather gone the way of
many towns these days; the butcher and the baker and the
candlestick maker have been replaced by the building society, the
bank and the newsagent. Even so, Darwin's conclusion holds true:
'He and his fellows will very possibly get in our way, or we shall
get in theirs; we shall often curse the crowd, and wish whole-
heartedly that golf was less popular in St Andrews. Nevertheless it
is that utter self abandonment to golf that gives the place its
attractiveness.' Never did this apply more than now, with the Ryder
Cup upon us.

At the top of Martet Street, the group made its way down
City Road and then back into Golf Place. They stood at Martyrs
Monument, which was erected in 1842 and dedicated to the
Protestants who were executed in St Andrews for their religious
beliefs. The small valley below is called Bow Butts, and opposite is
Witches Hill, where those accused of witchcraft were burned
during the period following the Reformation. Just below the cliff is
Witch Lake, where many of the accused were thrown, to suffer the
cruellest fate: if they floated they were witches; if they drowned
they were innocent. In 1856, a major storm in St Andrews Bay
washed up piles of bones on the beach.

The Golf Museum, which is situated just behind the clubhouse,
gave many wives a chance to reflect upon their husbands'
achievements. Almost all of them were featured in the museum in
some way. Many had given clubs commemorating famous
victories and these were now on show. The museum traces the
history of the game from its earliest roots and naturally and quite
rightly dwells on the considerable part that St Andrews in
particular and the east coast of Scotland in general have played in
the development of the sport.

One of the showcase displays honoured Faldo's Open victory
earlier in the year at his favourite course, Muirfield. A Mizuno bag
with his name written all over it was placed alongside a life-size
cardboard cut-out of Faldo, and encased in a trophy cabinet
behind was the pitching wedge with which he so brilliantly played
a stroke from the side of the 72nd green, the ball nestling stone
dead to signify victory.

Actually, the whole truth was a little more prosaic. It wasn't the pitching wedge that Faldo had used but an exact copy. The wedge he had deployed at Muirfield was still in its owner's bag, ready to do more sterling service.

The Gala Ball began with a champagne reception at 6.45 p.m. It was a black tie affair. It was held in St Andrews Town Hall, a splendidly fitting venue for such an occasion. Two hundred and twenty people had been squeezed inside – which, if truth be told, was rather too many for such an occasion. Everyone, it seemed, wanted to go to the Ball.

By 7.30 p.m. the reception area was crowded and full of the sound of laughter and conversation. The people there represented every section of the golfing business and beyond. There were MPs, showbiz celebrities, lords, ladies and gentlemen. There was even a former President.

George Bush had returned from his calls of duty and was now back in St Andrews. Actually, it hadn't all been work. He had long held a desire to see the Highlands of Scotland and so a helicopter tour had duly been arranged to escort him. It had been everything he hoped for, and now he related his experiences in the company of the captain of the Royal and Ancient Golf Club of St Andrews and a couple of local dignitaries. Several discreet bodyguards watched and waited.

A couple of European golfers had turned up and would stay for the week to give their colleagues moral support. Sam Torrance was never happier than when being involved in this biennial fixture. It had made his name and he had never forgotten it even if, in truth, some of his subsequent performances had been found wanting. But Torrance was a great supporter, a great patriot, and Jacklin was delighted to have him along. He had thought for a moment of making him vice-captain but Rees had to be the choice.

Mark James was also there, with his wife, Jane. Officially he was in attendance to represent the European tour's tournament committee but he would have gone anyway, and as a former Ryder Cup player on six occasions a place would have been found for him. James was perfect for this sort of gathering, and his dry sense of humour kept his table amused all evening. He was quite a revelation to two of the people around him, who had never guessed he would be like this. They had seen his rather dour image on television and thought this reflected his personality. But they were delighted to discover that nothing could have been further from the truth. One asked James what was the worst thing that had happened to him. Was it a 3-ft putt that had cost him the English Open? Was it failure to qualify for that year's Ryder Cup team? 'Actually, it was planting my bean sprouts too early one season and watching them all die of frost,' he replied.

The golf equipment companies were represented by presidents or vice-presidents or chairmen or deputy chairmen, depending on from which side of the Atlantic the firm originated. The sponsors of European tour events were also there, plus officials from all of golf's leading bodies.

By 7.45 p.m. everyone had located their seats and the gathering rose for the arrival of the two teams and their wives. They arrived in four enormous black limousines and were clapped every step of their journey to their places on two top tables. The players were wearing black ties too, the first time this had happened for many years. Some were not happy about this; no prizes for guessing their names.

Torrance and his wife Suzanne were seated on the table closest to the European team. Torrance kept turning round to share a laugh and a joke with his close friend, Woosnam. It was clear to all who witnessed this little scene that Torrance would have given quite a lot to have been sitting next to the Welshman, rather than behind him.

The meal was a suitably lavish affair. Each country that was represented in the European side supplied a course. The guests began with Scottish oak-smoked salmon, which, as one can imagine, went down very well with those present from the host country. Then came a thick Irish vegetable soup.

The main course was roast sirloin of English beef with green peppercorns, raisins and cognac, potatoes, and a selection of vegetables. A Bavarian raspberry cream with almond sauce was next, which Langer, at least, enjoyed. Snead thought it disgusting. So did Cotton. 'How are we supposed to eat this? We're athletes. We should be eating healthy food,' he argued. Cotton left his portion untouched. Faldo happily ate it for him.

By this time most people had been beaten into submission but there were still some who had reserved a space for the Welsh course, which was a selection of cheeses, including Caerphilly, of course. One of these was Faldo, who had a large chunk of each.

The Spanish course? That was served all night: Campo Viejo for those who liked white wine; a lovely 1988 Marqués de Murrieta rioja for those who preferred red.

After the meal it was the turn of the two captains to do their party tricks. The protocol demanded that they introduce their players to the gathering of distinguished guests. This might seem a very straightforward thing but it had produced some fun and games in the past. Once, a captain of the then Great Britain and Ireland team had gone on and on about the achievements of each of his players. His opposite number listened to it all, yawned, and then stood and asked the audience to reserve its applause for his team until the end. When they were all standing, he said, simply: 'Ladies and gentlemen, the United States Ryder Cup team, the finest golfers in the world.' The applause was overwhelming and many believe that the British and Irish team was beaten there and then.

In truth there wasn't much psychology attempted on this occasion. Jacklin and Hagen had too much respect for one another. Hagen stood up first, and said: 'Mr President, Lords, distinguished guests, it would be wrong for me to introduce my players as the finest golfers in the world but not for me to say it is the finest team ever to have represented the United States. I am very proud of all of them, and they've all worked very hard to be in front of you tonight. We're very aware of the special place the Ryder Cup holds in the sporting calendar and we will live up to its spirit. There's no need for me to list all of their achievements. For one thing, if I was to do that I would be here all night! But I will ask each of them to stand as I introduce him by name.' Each of the American team waved to the audience and bowed gently as he was called, and then Hagen ended this little formality by saying: 'I give you the United States Ryder Cup team.' The applause was warm and affectionate, and Hagen beamed his approval.

Jacklin stood and made a similar speech. But he couldn't resist little reminders of his team's prowess as he went along. Faldo was introduced as the current Open champion. Lyle, Langer, Olazabal and Woosnam were all talked of as Masters champions. And then came the finale. Jacklin said: 'Last, but certainly not least, three times Open champion and twice a Masters winner, and certainly the greatest Ryder Cup golfer that I've ever seen, Severiano Ballesteros.' Jacklin had calculated that this would bring the house down and he was right. Ballesteros loved it too, of course, waving with his right arm to every corner of the room. His team-mates clapped as well. Several of the American team looked annoyed but not Hagen. He smiled broadly at his opposing number, as if to say: 'Nice one, Jacko. Wish I'd have thought of that.'

The cabaret began at 10 p.m., after the loyal toast, which was proposed by the captain of the Professional Golfers' Association. The cabaret was performed by the comedian Bruce Forsyth and the singer Chris de Burgh. Both had long been part of the showbiz golfing scene and regularly participated in pro-ams held on the day before European tour events. Forsyth had a home on the Wentworth estate.

It has become a standing joke that every comedian over the age of 50 loves and reveres golf and every one under 30 makes fun of the fact. Whatever, Forsyth was perfect for this night and this gathering. His timing was superb. Invariably he would select one of the players and talk of his achievements and what he'd done for the game and then the punchline would bring him back down to earth, and have the audience convulsed in laughter. For example: 'And then there's the American captain, Walt Hagen. I can call you Walt, can't I, now that you're in Hollywood? Think of all he has done for the game. Go on, think . . .' Forsyth went up and shook Hagen's hand and with genuine warmth wished him the best of luck for the week. It was a polished performance by Forsyth and went down well with everyone, which was more than could be said for the singer who followed. De Burgh was too loud for some and too shrill for others. It was quite a blessing when he finally got round to 'Lady in Red', because that meant it must be time for him to pack up.

It was now 10.45 p.m. and for the distinguished guests there was still dancing to come with music by the Ray McVay orchestra. For the teams it was time to go home. The trouble was, it was hard for them to rise out of their chairs. They were surrounded by people clamouring for autographs. Hagen loved it at first, and particularly when it was a woman who requested his signature. But then a crush of a different kind developed. At one point, the pushing was such around the American team that someone fell against the back of Nelson, causing him in turn to fall forward against the table. That was enough for Hagen. He called a stop to all autograph signing. His face had changed now and he raised his voice to signal to the crowd around the table that the proceedings were at an end. He told his team to follow him to the limousines that were waiting outside. Nelson was shaken but unhurt, but it was an unfortunate end to a fine evening.

Under normal circumstances Hagen would have stayed and told his team to go on without him. After all, the last woman to request his signature was gorgeous. But the incident led him to changing a lifetime's habit of enjoying the moment.

The European team followed soon after. Most players and their wives were extremely tired. Cotton had fallen asleep during de Burgh's routine. Of the Americans, Lema was still wide awake, but then he often was when surrounded by company and drink.

When they returned to the hotel it was just Lema and his captain who filed into the Hagen Room for one nightcap. In normal circumstances both would have preferred to have had this drink in the bar downstairs but both had seen enough of a crowd for one night.

Hagen was closest to Lema of all his players. Here was a kindred spirit. Hagen had heard the whispers in certain quarters that Lema had been chosen out of favouritism, ahead of Demaret and Floyd and the rest. But the accusation never really stood up and, in any case, Hagen had a totally clear conscience about it all. Yes, Lema was his friend. But how could you leave out your worst enemy if he'd proved that he could beat all the best golfers in the Open at St Andrews?

'Are you ready to spring any great surprises tomorrow, Haig?', Lema asked.

'Nope. Everyone will line up on Friday regardless of how the alternate shots go in the morning. Clearly, who plays both morning and afternoon depends on how the first series is going and who's on form and who ain't.'

'Who's playing in the morning?'

'You and Tom for a start. You look a good combination.'

'We are a good combination. Neither of us is very long but we've got something.'

'I plan to play Nicklaus and Hogan at least three out of the four games. I just hope Ben's legs hold up. He and Jack look a frighteningly good combination to me. I can't think of anyone, not even Seve and Ollie, who would relish taking them on. Seve and Ollie are something, though, aren't they? That was quite a touch of Jacklin's tonight, wasn't it? He's a great captain and he knows that Seve responds to his call. He knows he's not intimidated by the responsibility but inspired by it. But I'd still back Ben and Jack to win.'

'Are you sorry not to be playing?'

'Sure. I enjoyed my practice on Tuesday. It brought back all the memories, you know? But I'm not the player I was. I can't cut it at both ends any more, Tony.'

The pair smiled at one another. They had enjoyed a few good times together on tour, and a few whiskies. Now their glasses were drained and they decided to have one more before Hagen really was going to put his captain's hat on and order his player to go to his room.

It was 11.30 p.m. Back at the Town Hall, the party was in full swing. Most of the black ties were now in jacket pockets, or certainly not as neat around the neck as before. Torrance was telling everyone who cared to listen that Europe was going to win and that he was heartbroken not to be part of the side.

The Murrieta continued to flow, not to mention the late-bottled vintage port and the Hennessy VSOP, and the miniature bottles of Johnnie Walker Black Label that had been placed on every table had in many instances been opened and enjoyed.

The Jacklin Room was empty, apart from a waiter who would be there all night in case anyone had any need of anything. Indeed, he had been on his own all evening, for no one had entered the room upon returning from the Gala Ball.

At least his counterpart in the Hagen Room had been partly employed. But now his trade for the evening was about to hit the road as well. Both Lema and his captain slept very soundly indeed.

4

Thursday:
The Opening Ceremony

WITH THE TAKING of the Ryder Cup to St Andrews a new era for the competition had begun. The infighting was now a thing of the past. The event had ceased to be a political golf ball and was no longer shamelessly used to promote whatever suited either the Professional Golfers' Association or the European tour.

True, the Old Course was hardly the most suitable venue in many respects. The 25,000 all-ticket crowd were clearly going to encounter some horrendous problems over the first two days if their intentions were to follow the golf rather than let the golf come to them.

Accommodation was difficult too, with many people staying in Edinburgh simply because nothing closer was available.

But few people objected, because the whole exercise just felt right and nothing is more important to golfers than a sense that the spirit of the game is being observed. A Ryder Cup at St Andrews fitted perfectly into this philosophy. Not that commerce was being totally ignored. Prices for hospitality units were verging on the exorbitant, yet such was the magnetic appeal of both the venue and the event that companies had been happy to foot the bill.

The tented village was lavish and its centrepiece was a vast structure, even bigger than the media centre, where the golf industry paraded its wares. This was turning out to be a big day for the exhibitors. It was raining. In fact, it was pouring down. For hardy golf fans, that was no deterrent to walking the miles to follow the fortunes of their favourite players but a great many were happy to accept the relative comforts on offer and take a look at what the industry itself was selling.

The elements deposited on to the makeshift roof gave a warm glow of satisfaction to those sheltering inside. A particularly popular stand was the one selling umbrellas. The delighted owner had sold out by lunchtime and was desperately ordering fresh supplies.

The big manufacturers had taken much of the space available in the centre aisles. Two of the biggest had given over much of their stands to supposedly revolutionary new clubs that they had launched at the Trade Show in Birmingham the previous November. Several players contracted to the respective companies had made guest appearances this week to help the promotion. In truth, both manufacturers were recycling old ideas. It's hard to come up with new ones in a sport that's been around for so many centuries.

In fact, some of the most interesting stands were to be found tucked away in the tent's outer edges, where the prices had been more accommodating. Here were the book-keepers and the specialist club makers and the agents trying to sell golf holidays in the last places that anyone would have thought of. The inventors – some of whom were harmless cranks and some genuine innovators – were here too. It was wise to check these people out. Once, at a Ryder Cup in Houston, two journalists had been approached as they idly walked through such a tent as this. Their pursuer was rather strange looking with his goatee beard. He claimed he had invented a revolutionary new putter and he gave the journalists two examples each of his product. Of course they dismissed him with barely a thought. Neither got on with the putters they had received and duly gave them away. This was not the wisest thing to have done in view of the fact that Karsten Solheim, for it was he, really had come up with a revolutionary new putter, the Ping Anser, and the two journalists went on to rue the day they carelessly gave away a present that would fetch a tidy sum were it sold today at a Sotheby's auction.

On show at St Andrews were both the old and the new. On one stand was a golf antiques expert, who was giving advice to customers on what to look for to discover valuable golf paintings and golf clubs. Next door was a would-be Solheim, with a futuristic sand wedge and the rather outrageous claim that even the poorest bunker player could get down in 2 on at least seven occasions out of ten – always presuming, of course, that they were using his club, which had at least been checked and accepted by the Royal and Ancient, if not his claims by the Advertising Standards Authority.

One stand was occupied by the National Hole in One Association, whose president was the perfect person to talk about such things since he had had no fewer than fifty in competitions alone. He was expanding his British business. Passers-by were keen to find out how he was such a lucky so-and-so. 'You think it's all luck?', he would reply, tantalizingly. Actually he didn't really know why he had been so blessed. It certainly wasn't the quality of his golf: he was no better than a medium handicapper. But what he did claim was that he knew as soon as he struck a shot whether it was going into the hole or not. It was like a movie playing in his mind, he said. He could visualize the shot, and knew where the ball would bounce and where it would end up.

As the morning progressed with no sign of the rain relenting, the tent filled up until there was hardly any space to move freely along the crowded centre passageways.

In the entire history of the Ryder Cup there have only been two holes in one. Nick Faldo had one of them. It wasn't on his mind at this minute. Keeping dry and swinging smoothly were the current preoccupation.

After two magnificent autumn days the weather had certainly broken and the 'auld grey toun' was matched by a sky of a similar colour. The rain had started falling from first light and wasn't going to end until the tide went out in mid-afternoon.

The Americans were first out today. Snead's face was so grumpy it would have frightened little children. To be fair, the only people who wore broad smiles were the waterproof manufacturers, who were delighted to see their products getting such a public airing.

For the organizers this was the stuff of nightmares. The opening ceremony was due to start at 4.30 p.m. The rain was scheduled to end at 4 p.m. They just hoped the weather forecasters would be right. As it was, they would face a heck of a rush to get all the tables and chairs in place in the thirty minutes that they hoped to have available. For the players, it was less of a problem. True, practice had been curtailed to as many shots as were necessary to feel loose-limbed and ready to play. But the rain just drained through the sand-based links like water down a plughole. The only real inconvenience was the greens, which were a mite slower owing to the fact that the greenkeeping staff had been unable to cut them that morning.

Indeed, a number of players were delighted to see the Old Course displaying another of its moods. Ideally they would have liked to have played it in a stiff breeze but the promise was for the wind to pick up as the day progressed and blow the rain clouds away.

So they set out once more, with just one practice round to go, to hone and fine-tune, to watch and to learn.

A breeze is certainly what Palmer would have picked given the choice. He was at that stage in his career where the untamed power that had so thrilled a generation had passed and in its place was a golfer whose thickening brow lines indicated the wealth of experience that he now possessed. Since St Andrews is a course where driving length rarely proves a particular advantage he felt sure that this, his last Ryder Cup, could be a successful one. His record in the competition was one of which he felt intensely proud. It was better than that of Nicklaus, for example, and any time he was ahead of the Golden Bear could only be good news. Palmer knew that the Europeans feared him too. Cotton called him the most popular golfer in the world and Jacklin himself had expressed disquiet over whether the Palmer factor might dissipate the loyalties of the home crowd.

Nevertheless Arnie, as he was known to all and sundry, could feel the passing of the years, both in the loss of vigour when he awoke each morning and in the steady loss of hearing in both ears that would necessitate the use of a medical aid before many more seasons passed.

Yet as the hair went greyer and thinner and his golfing skills gradually diminished so Palmer found no decrease in his fan club, as Cotton acknowledged. The fabled army had just grown old with him. They had taken the highly plausible view: there was only one Arnold Palmer.

The great man had wondered whether he might be paired off with one of the younger players on this occasion, for he felt he had lots to offer as a patriarch. As it turned out, Hagen partnered him with the one player in either side who was older. Great names, great reputations: Hagen felt, as he did with the Hogan–Nicklaus combination, that the opposition would start a hole down.

Certainly the pair were alike in many ways. His partner, Sarazen, remained a gambler on the golf course as well as off it. He was also immune to the teachings of the so-called golf gurus who had crept into the sport. Someone like Faldo might have rebuilt his game from scratch but Sarazen would always stick with what he had. And what he had certainly worked for him even in these, the sunset years of his career.

Sarazen had been asked often enough about his grip and the swing that he built so steadfastly around it. In a long piece in that morning's *Daily Mail* he had talked about technique and what he believed was the game's secret: 'Golf requires a lot of practice; an awful lot, in fact. I really like to practise. I recently heard a fellow say that if he spent three or four or five hours practising with one club then the game ceased to be a pleasure and became work. Maybe that's true if you don't like to practise. To me it's interesting to see how close to the pin I can come with 100 balls at 100 yards and then from 75 yards and so on. It is this kind of practice that enables me to play my shots accurately. I have practised six or seven hours at a stretch and all with one club. That is why, when I am about to make a shot, I know exactly what I can do with the club I am about to use. I know whether I can stop the ball 2 ft from the pin at a certain distance because practice has taught me just how much effort I must use to accomplish the end I seek. I am sure always of every shot I make.

'Of course, the best of them will go wrong at times and when this happens I realize that I have neglected my practice. Then I go out and remedy the defect and I practise until I am absolutely confident that I can do what I want to do.'

Clearly he would need to put in some serious hours after the final practice round. Sarazen and Palmer couldn't hold a candle to Nelson and Watson, who took the money. Watson was really starting to enjoy himself. His years of dominance might have come to an end but he was hitting the ball from tee to green probably better than in his prime. The difference was on the greens. He could still hole more than his fair share but he knew that the imperious confidence he once held in this area of the game had long gone and it was all downhill from now on in. Yet under

Nelson's watching brief he had managed to hold on to something, maybe for one week or maybe not, and perhaps just for a fleeting moment he was experiencing the return of some of that old belief.

Snead and Mangrum managed to beat Trevino and Casper. Snead therefore recouped the money that he had lost in the opening game to Nelson and Watson. It was a straw for him to clutch on to and he duly did.

Hagen spent a long time watching this match, talking to his players before scuttling away in his buggy. It would help him decide his final strategy for the morning foursomes.

The Europeans were more relaxed. The best golf came from Faldo and Oosterhuis, as the former demonstrated once more his peerless capacity to prevail in adverse weather conditions. It was as if the addition of an extra burden concentrated his mind. Faldo was round in 66 with just one bogey at the 17th to set against the seven birdies including five in a dazzling outward half of 31 strokes.

Ballesteros and Olazabal beat Langer and Cotton, which at least cheered up the former pair, if not Jacklin. Brown and Lyle struggled. The former blamed it on the latter, considering him a wet-weather wimp. Nearly all of the players retired to their rooms or suites for long, hot baths. They were to meet at 2.30 p.m. The dress rehearsal was almost at an end.

What goes through a player's mind as he lies there and wonders whether his captain is about to choose him to play in the opening foursomes the following morning in the Ryder Cup?

In a typical week, after the day's golf is over, most will try to forget the game for a while before returning to do some practice. But there was no respite now. To a man, they all wondered what their captain had in store. Several, of course, knew they were certainties to play but this did not stop them from speculating on who else would be playing and who would be dropped.

What was certain was that no one was going to go up to his

captain and ask to be excused from duty. All felt they were playing well enough not to have to do that.

After the long soak the players changed into their team uniforms. The American team wore rustic red Ralph Lauren blazers and grey trousers accompanied by a tie that was a tasteful adaptation of the United States flag. The Europeans wore dark green blazers made by the tour's clothing sponsor, Hugo Boss.

In the Jacklin Room, the captain was waiting for his team as they entered. They made themselves comfortable on the four leather sofas the room contained and which had been pulled into a semicircle shape for the purposes of the meeting. Jacklin sat opposite them.

He spoke. 'Gentlemen, we've all been in this situation before and we all know the score. The time for talking is almost over. We'll have an informal dinner tonight but then the serious work begins. I feel the week is going as well as we could have asked. I've watched you all over the last couple of days and I've talked to you out on the golf course and I've talked to your playing partners to see how they're feeling and how the formations are working out.

'And I've decided to go with my gut instinct, and stick with the pairings we've had all week. I know, Eric, you've had reservations about playing with Sandy but you two seem to be gelling into quite a formidable partnership and you will surprise the Americans.

'Everyone will play tomorrow. There's no one who's performing badly enough to miss out on a whole day's play. Who plays both morning and afternoon we'll have to see after a few holes tomorrow. Eric and Sandy, and Henry and Bernhard will be missing tomorrow morning and so will have that time to prepare for the afternoon fourballs, when Eric and Sandy will be first out. In the morning we're going to lead with Barnesy and Bernard. I think you two will probably find yourselves up against Hogan and Nicklaus but you'll have the crowd on your side from the start and if you get off to a flier then it could well set the tone for the morning. The crowd would certainly then lift everyone else.

'Nick and Oosty will follow and then Woosie and Christy. Seve and Ollie will play the anchor role.

'As I say, I think we've got everything to look forward to. I think everyone will play at least twice over the first two days and probably three times. Anyone got anything they want to say?'

Inevitably there were murmurs of discontent from three of the four players who had been left out of the opening series. Lyle was the only one who accepted the captain's decision without comment. For a start, Lyle didn't like foursomes. For another, he didn't think Jacklin rated him that highly as a Ryder Cup player. He had set his sights on playing once each day, and any addition would come as a bonus.

'It's bloody stupid,' said Cotton. 'Bernhard and I are made to play foursomes golf. We could take on anybody!' There was probably some truth in that, Jacklin thought to himself. He silently acknowledged that he was taking a gamble but then how on earth were they to beat such a formidable American team if gambles were not taken?

'Barnesy, Bernard, do you have any thoughts about going out first?' Jacklin asked.

'Delighted,' they choroused.

Barnes went on to add: 'I totally agree with your strategy, and we're ready to take on anybody. We'll give anyone a game and a half.'

Jacklin could see that Brown was stewing. 'Eric, you feel you should be playing, I know, but there's a long way to go. You'll get your chance, I promise you. Your attitude is spot on. We need you if we're going to win.'

Dai Rees chipped in with a few words too. It had been a quiet week for the diminutive Welshman. There hadn't been much for him to do. He had been determined to arrive at St Andrews bearing no outward anguish at Jacklin for not including him in the side and had earned much admiration among the rest of the team for his attitude. In any case, he was highly respected, and Brown was among his admirers. Rees knew this. He told Brown, 'You'll be a star this week, Eric, I've no doubt about that. Foursomes is not your game. We need you strong for later in the event. You've not lost to a Yankee in singles matches yet and I don't think you're going to start here.'

Brown was placated. Just.

———————

Across the hallway, some three doors further down, Hagen was addressing his players in similar fashion. If anything, his task was that much harder. In the European team, despite Cotton's protestations, there were four outstanding foursomes partnerships, and Jacklin, even though he had some inner doubts, would have been foolhardy to have opened with any other.

But the American team's talents were more uniform. Mangrum and Snead would play, of course, and Hogan and Nicklaus had every chance of making the starting line-up too, although there had to be some doubts whether Hogan's legs would withstand the demands of five matches.

Hagen was busily explaining this to his team. Like Jacklin he told his players that all of them would get a game the following day. 'This may be the first American side that has travelled across the Atlantic with no obvious flaws. So you'll all play at least three times. I'm going to put out Jack and Ben first in the morning. The last thing we need is for the other lot to get off to a cracking start and the sight of Hogan and Nicklaus is as good a way as I can think of for nipping that in the bud.

'Tom and Byron will follow and then you, Tom [pointing at Kite], and Tony. Lloyd and Sam will play last. Gentlemen, I have to tell you it's been hard making up my mind about these partnerships but I felt Arnold and Gene, and Lee and Billy will make two great fourballs pairings and I'm keen to make sure that we stay as fresh as we can over the course of three demanding days. I think we have the edge over the opposition in strength in depth and we have to remember that Sunday is the most important day of all.'

Somewhat to his surprise, the players in front of him did not openly disagree with his choices. Palmer and Sarazen had no inclination to play five matches in three days. Trevino and Casper had been partners in previous Ryder Cups without any great success but they saw no reason for that and liked the idea of playing fourballs golf.

As the meeting broke up, and the players pressed a bell and gave their lunch orders to their waiter, who arrived in an instant, Hagen swept across the room to call Hogan to one side. 'Ben, I know you don't like to talk about your legs and all, but I need to know whether you think you can play all five matches. You know I think you and Jack are the top players in either side and I want you two to play all the time if you can. I know Jack can go the distance. He's young. But I want you to tell me what you think.'

'Hagen, I think you should ask me after I've played twice tomorrow,' Hogan replied.

———————

Jacklin and Hagen met up as they had planned and went in the same chauffeured car together to the media tent. It was to be a joint interview. The pairings were not due to be made public until the opening ceremony but they followed the time-honoured practice of giving them earlier to the press on condition that the strict 4.30 p.m. embargo was adhered to.

'I'll tell you mine if you tell me yours,' Hagen said, laughing. They were accompanied by officials from both the Professional Golfers' Association and the PGA of America, and the team sheets were duly swapped.

'I thought you'd go with Jack and Ben first,' Jacklin said.

Hagen replied: 'It'll be some match against Brian and Bernard. I see you've left Eric out. That'll please some of our boys. He's a cussed son of a bitch, isn't he?'

'He just doesn't like you Yankees,' Jacklin said. 'No place for Arnie, either?'

'Arnie's time will come.'

So the two captains were escorted into the media interview room where the press officer read out the four matches that would open this Ryder Cup:

> Barnes, Gallacher v. Hogan, Nicklaus
> Faldo, Oosterhuis v. Nelson, Watson
> Woosnam, O'Connor v. Kite, Lema
> Ballesteros, Olazabal v. Mangrum, Snead

The press officer explained that both captains were on tight deadlines because of the opening ceremony, but they would answer brief questions. Both were asked to explain their thinking and how they thought the draw had panned out.

Jacklin went first. 'Well, it's very interesting, isn't it? We expected Walter to lead off with Hogan and Nicklaus, and Brian and Bernard volunteered to take them on. They'll be relishing the fact that such a match is now going to take place.

'But they're all impossible to predict. There'll be sixteen world-class players on view and it's going to come down to who holes a few putts. What I can tell you is that my fellas are in terrific heart and I expect us to come out on top at the end of it. Yes, I expect us to win.'

'Will the four who were not chosen play in the afternoon and how did they take being left out?'

'Eric and Henry were absolutely thrilled as you can imagine. No, seriously, there were a few mutterings of protest but then you'd hope for that sort of response. Everyone is itching to play their part and I'd have been disappointed if they had been totally happy about the situation. But make no mistake: all twelve players will have every chance to influence the destiny of this match.'

'Walter?'

'I don't think there are any surprises in the eight guys that Tony is putting out tomorrow morning and my hunch is that the other four will play in the fourballs in the afternoon. If I was in his shoes I think I would have done exactly the same. I can only agree with Tony in how I think the matches will shape up. Obviously the top match could well have a bearing on how everything goes.

'We're here to win but equally we know we're going to have to play awfully well to achieve that. I'm happy for everyone to know that all twelve of my players will get a game tomorrow. I think it would be dreadfully unfair on someone if they didn't play. They're all here because they are the twelve best Americans and they deserve the chance to show what they can do. On the question of whether the four were upset at being left out I disagree here slightly with Tony. The guys weren't upset because they know they will be playing in the afternoon and they know this is going to be perhaps the most gruelling Ryder Cup of all time and that five matches in three days is asking a lot of anyone.'

'Are you saying that none of your players will play in all five matches?'

'I am not saying that at all. But I don't think many will and I wouldn't be surprised at all if it turns out that none of my team play any more than four games.'

'What about you, Tony?'

'I'll be absolutely astonished if two players in particular in my team don't play in all the matches and I would expect three or four to do so. Walter is right when he says the demands placed upon the players are enormous but they've done it before and I expect them to do it again. It's going to be a great occasion and they're positively straining at the leash. And besides, they can sleep all next week if they want.'

'When did you decide on your pairings, Tony?'

'I've had them in my mind for about a week now. Certainly before I came out here. I talked it through with Dai and with Seve and Nick Faldo and they were in agreement. I think we've got four natural pairings and two potentially very strong ones in Brown and Lyle, and Cotton and Langer.'

'Any last thoughts as to how the match will go?'

'I really wouldn't have tried to combine what I'm doing in America with this if I didn't think we could win. Obviously we lost last time and so that makes us even more determined on this occasion. I'm just looking forward to it. I think we've got a good team and maybe the home advantage will just swing things our way a little. I'm not going to get much sleep but, hell, it's going to be great fun.'

Hagen said: 'I'm really glad in a way that the match is now almost upon us. The hype and the build-up has been something else and I'm really ready to go watch these guys play. Is playing at home a big advantage? Sure it is, and especially at a place like here at St Andrews where local knowledge is such a help. And most of our guys only play the bump-and-run shot that's needed here at one tournament a year. It's hard for them to adapt. But I'm confident they will adapt. We've got nine British Open champions and that to me says that they'll adapt.'

The foreshortened press interview had come to an end. Jacklin's relish was obvious. Hagen had a broad smile too. The pair shook hands and wished each other luck. They volunteered to return after the opening ceremony but few of the journalists thought that would be necessary. Everyone had many words to write and their offices were demanding that they deliver them in good time. No one wanted to be revising their thoughts and possibly rewriting after the opening ceremony.

And so the two captains left, in their Sunday best outfits. The umbrellas that they had carried with them into the media tent were unnecessary as they emerged back into the light. The rain had stopped on cue. The skies were clearing a little. It wasn't going to be sunny for the opening ceremony but at least it would be dry.

————

The ceremony took place in front of the 18th green. By now the stand behind the final hole and the ones to the right of the first fairway were both overflowing. In the buildings along Links Place, people were straining from every window or vantage point for a view. In the Big Room in the clubhouse of the Royal and Ancient, every seat was filled, which was hardly surprising since the bay window overlooking the first tee offered one of the best views of all.

The ceremony was a simple affair. Either side of a central podium were two rows of chairs containing twenty-four seats for each team. Twelve were obviously reserved for the respective players and twelve for the leading officials from America and Europe.

This latter body of men were already in place and they included, among the Americans, George Bush. This had necessitated quite a security operation since the Americans insisted on waving a metal detector over every spectator who was either sitting in the stand or watching from Links Place. Security guards watched every window but their presence was not overbearing and soon all thoughts were back on the occasion as a local band entertained the crowd with a selection of tunes and then overhead the Red Arrows roared their own salute, flying over in perfect formation.

And then out came the teams. Side by side they emerged from the clubhouse, came down the steps and across the first tee and then they split into two to take their places either side of the podium. The reception was predictably enthusiastic.

The national anthems were played. In Europe's case, this, of course, took some time since there were a number of anthems to play. The players took their seats and the executive director of the Professional Golfers' Association made his way to the podium. He introduced the association's president, who extended the hand of friendship to the Americans and spoke of his great hopes for the match and the occasion. He told of the great honour he felt that among the visiting dignitaries should be a former President of the United States.

The executive director returned to the podium after his short address and called upon the American captain to introduce his team to the assembled gathering.

Hagen said: 'Mr President, Mr President of the PGA, ladies and gentlemen, it really is a great honour for me to be captain of what I believe to be the best team that has ever left American shores, and we dearly want to take the cup back with us. But I really believe that far more important than that is the fact that the game of golf should emerge only with credit this weekend. Looking around me at two great teams and knowing what knowledgeable galleries we're going to have, I can only think that is going to be the case. And if I may, this is America's team.'

Hagen read out all the names and each player stood up briefly and acknowledged the cheering of the crowds as his name was called. It was very clear who were the more popular American players, as Nicklaus and Watson got especially warm greetings, while the applause that followed the announcement of Palmer's name would prove to be louder than that afforded several European players.

Then it was Jacklin's turn. He said: 'Walter, we welcome you and your team, we really do. This is a competition for which we have waited for a long time and we know it is going to be really tough. But in my opinion, this cup down here [Jacklin pointed at the Ryder Cup in front of the podium] is coming home. Now, let me introduce my team.'

Just as he had at the Gala Ball Jacklin made a little more of the introductions than had Hagen. He introduced every player and then said how many times he had played in the Ryder Cup, as if to emphasize that little could faze them. He emphasized too the players' familiarity with their audience. 'Little Woosie', Ian Woosnam . . . things like that. Once more Ballesteros was left until last, where he got the biggest cheer of the afternoon.

The executive director then read out the pairings for the morning fourballs. As he read out the opening match the assembled throng collectively drew a sharp intake of breath. 'Yes, it's quite a match to look forward to, isn't it?', the executive director said.

Inevitably there was some disappointment among the Scots that Brown and Lyle had been left out.

The band played on, and the teams left the arena. The audience clapped them out, and then started filing out of their seats. The members in the R&A clubhouse ordered afternoon tea or a drop of Scotch. The tented village prepared itself for one last influx of people before closing time. The windows in Links Place were now once more closed to the chill and the people who lived or worked there went back to what they had been doing. For forty-five minutes the players had been there in front of them and this latest staging of the Ryder Cup had been declared officially open.

But now expectations were back on hold. The feast had been set but it would be sixteen or so hours yet before everyone could begin to satisfy their hunger.

Snead was hardly the only person whose first reaction to St Andrews was to think: 'Is this really the Home of Golf?' Many Americans in particular play it once and wonder what all the fuss is about. They go home with tales of how quaint the town is and how goddam awful the golf course is. Such is the persuasive power of word of mouth that when the 1989 Open Champion Mark Calcavecchia came back to defend his trophy the following year at St Andrews he thought he was about to set foot on the worst course in the world.

Even Bobby Jones, who was made a freeman of the town in later life and came out with one of the most extraordinarily corny lines of all time – 'If I could take out of my life all my experiences bar those at St Andrews I would still have led a full and rich life' – couldn't stand the place at first. Often it doesn't get much better on second or third viewing either. Sandy Lyle played it at least twenty times before he gained even the slightest appreciation.

The problem is that the course is very plain. It is a links course and yet the sea is only visible from the 1st and the 18th holes and not even then when the Open or, as in this case, the Ryder Cup comes to town since tented or grandstand acreage blocks all views. It has nothing like the dramatic aesthetic sweep of the holes at Turnberry that hug the Ayrshire coast. Neither are there the imposing sand dunes that line the fairways at Royal Birkdale nor the innate fairness that characterizes Muirfield. What is left, and what carries the visitor along, is its charm, its eccentricity and, most of all, its tradition.

But of course charm and eccentricity are relative things and if one doesn't see those qualities then one sees very little at all and one goes away considering the Old Course overrated and outdated. What I would characterize as charm and eccentricity are the many ways in which it breaks with accepted wisdom in course design. There are only two par 3s, for example, as against the usual four. There are only two par 5s, again when more typically there are four. Twelve of the holes share double greens, some of which are so massive that it would take a full sand wedge to get from one side of the green to the other.

And imagine an architect coming along today and designing a hole like the 1st! The land is as flat as a pancake with just a thin apology of a stream running in front of the green as protection: he would be laughed out of court. But, as the estate agents always say, location is everything. Stick St Andrews Bay to the right; line the left-hand side of the fairway with character-filled buildings; have the tee framed by the R&A clubhouse; it's less plain now. Its reputation as an easy starting hole is not always borne out either. During one round at the Dunhill Cup scores ranged from 2 to 7, including every figure in between.

Here endeth the first lesson: do not think St Andrews is as easy as it might first appear; do not be deceived into thinking it as wide open as it seems.

The key to success over the Old Course? Ballesteros described St Andrews as a place ideal for those who draw the ball, since all the trouble is on the right side.

All the players were in agreement that a good score was on if one avoided the notorious St Andrews bunkers, many of which are named and some of which were to add to that notoriety in the days ahead. Many of the bunkers are hidden, which has driven many a first-time visitor to distraction, and led people to deem the course unfair, sending them back home with knitted brows and dark tales. No one really knows quite why the bunkers were built in this way but perhaps the fact that the course used to be played in a clockwise direction and not, as currently, anticlockwise had something to do with it.

Such bunkers, of course, would not come as a surprise to the players in this Ryder Cup. All the caddies had them comprehensively charted in notebooks that were as valuable to them as a priceless painting is to an art collector. Not that such extensive knowledge meant that the players would entirely avoid visiting them, of course.

Cheape's Bunker on the 2nd hole is one especially to avoid. It comes into play off the drive and any thoughts of a par are dramatically diminished by any tee shot that finishes in the sand.

James Cheape, incidentally, was a rather odd laird who in 1894 extracted from St Andrews the right to go on the course to gather the shells which are characteristic of this corner of Fife. He crushed them and then used them on the paths of his nearby estate. His ancestors still live in the house, crushed shells and all.

The 3rd is one of the easiest holes on the course and most players would be looking for a birdie in reasonable conditions. The same cannot be said for the par 4 4th, which can be unreachable if played into anything above a breeze.

It is undeniable that fortune plays its full part at St Andrews. Few players can achieve a really low score without a fair portion. The 5th is a prime example. If the bunkers are avoided off the tee on this par 5 hole a possible birdie opportunity ensures, but a large hollow masks the front of the green. Will the good shot be killed by the slope or will it bound on? You plays your shot and you takes your chance.

Most players would be upset at spilling a shot at the 6th, which leads into the Loop, holes 7 to 11, where everyone is looking to pick up strokes. The 7th is an easy par 4; the short 8th an orthodox par 3; the par 4 9th is invariably drivable, as Jack Nicklaus had demonstrated in practice on the Tuesday; the par 4 10th is short too and no one should have more than a little pitch to the green.

The par 3 11th is an entirely different proposition altogether. Two bunkers, the Hill and the Strath, protect two sides of an awkward-shaped green and from either of them there is little chance of getting down in 2, such is their depth and the obstacle posed by a green that slopes severely from back to front.

Its yardage suggests that the 312-yard 12th should be easy but here again the green undulates to such a degree that it is difficult to get the ball close to the flag, whether it be with a huge drive or even with a pitching wedge after a 4 or 5 iron off the tree. All sorts of penalties await the badly struck drive, as one would expect.

Trouble on the 13th usually follows a sliced tee shot, where the Coffin Bunkers, which need no explanation as to why they got their name, duly lie. The hole shares its green with the 5th and, at ninety paces across, is the biggest of all at St Andrews.

The 14th is the second par 5 with out of bounds on the right of a flat fairway known as the Elysian Fields. The pot-hole Beardies

Bunkers lurk on the left. Why Beardies? Because the grass, for some reason, was difficult to cut in front of the bunkers and so was often left to grow. Many players aim down the 5th fairway here, which, if there is any wind against, leaves a long carry over Hell Bunker. This hazard got its name when one golfer, following a poor round, complained to Old Tom Morris that the only decent lie he had found was at the bottom of the bunker at the 14th and that he had been able to get a 4 wood at it. The next day, a puce-faced Morris sent out a work crew who chiselled away until there was not even the remotest possibility that someone could hit a wood from there.

Another area to avoid on this 567-yard hole is the hollow in front of the green. Many a 3-putt has been taken from there.

In theory the 15th should be a straightforward par 4 with little to concern a player off the tee or to the green. Not so the 16th, where the Principal's Nose Bunker has been set down slap bang in the middle of the fairway. A preposterous place to put a bunker, some might say, and the locals would not totally disagree. For the bunker owes its name not to the fact it bears nasal characteristics but because of something altogether more meaningful. It concerns the South Street family home of that appropriately named peer, Sir Hugh Playfair. Sir Hugh's father, a principal of St Andrews University, added a front porch to this house in 1810. The local residents were not best pleased. They detested it, and dubbed it The Principal's Nose. Sir Hugh had the thing pulled down in 1844, and so the offending name was transferred to something else that got up the noses of the St Andreans: the bunker in the middle of the 16th fairway.

Many of the twenty-four players who stepped on to the 17th tee during the Ryder Cup did so in the full knowledge that they were about to encounter what they believed to be the toughest par 4 in the world. The drive is bad enough, with nothing to aim at but the grounds of the Old Course Hotel. But the second shot is so difficult as to call into question the fairness of it all. Few players will have less than a midiron to the green, and what they have to aim at is the merest sliver of a target, with a hollow protecting the front, plus the notorious Road Hole Bunker, with the road itself deterring any who go long.

Hagen was asked about it and replied that it wasn't the toughest par 4 at all; it was the easiest par 5. 'I would never dream of telling my players to play holes in a certain way but any player who adopts the strategy of aiming for the front apron of this green is doing the right thing by me,' he said. Not treating it as a par 4 is certainly one way of looking at it. Suffice to say that anyone who stands on the 17th tee knows either that there is still hope or there is still much to negotiate before victory can be claimed.

The 18th does not just share a fairway with the 1st: it shares its setting. That is just as well because this, in theory, is a terribly plain hole with which to finish a Ryder Cup. Think of the drama of the 18th at The Belfry, where anything can happen. At St Andrews it's the 17th where anything can happen. Yet think a little deeper: the final hole on the Old Course has witnessed its own fair share of amazing happenings. The location terrifies the timid but gladdens the senses of those with fortitude. And maybe then it is not a bad finishing hole at all and perhaps, even, the perfect finishing hole for a Ryder Cup. For what is such competition all about if not to identify those with strong minds and big hearts?

In the media tent the journalists were continuing the job of whetting everyone's appetite. This was not easy. It was the final preview day, and as ever it was a bitch. What do you say when everything appears to have already been said? What do you write when a couple of billion words have already been written? A small group of hacks stared at an empty computer screen for what must have been an hour or more. Several wrote a couple of paragraphs and then pressed the delete button.

Most of the tabloids ended up taking the easy way out, as their golf correspondents just wrote long pieces saying one of two things. It was either: 'This weekend the Ryder Cup is coming home. It's going to be yanked out of American hands.' Or: 'The American team of stars are once more about to earn their stripes. Europe has no chance.' There was more inclination to lean towards the latter view than the former, and this was reflected by the bookmakers. The Americans were firm favourites to achieve another win.

There was a branch of bookmakers on site in the tented village and it had proved a popular spot with punters all week. Now it was absolutely crowded as people had a flutter not only on the overall result but also on individual matches. Most popular of all here was the top match. Very favourable odds indeed were offered on Barnes and Gallacher emerging triumphant and many patriotic Scots couldn't resist taking on the bookmakers' pessimism.

———————

It was dark. What to do now before the sky broke and let in some light and the morning hour arrived? The players went back to their hotel and Cotton and Faldo to their respective masseurs. Cotton was suffering from some lower back pain. This was hardly new. He had suffered such agonies for twenty years or so, owing to the irregular curvature of his spine brought on through all the years of practice. With his bad back and his bad stomach Cotton was not in a good way but he had learned to live with discomfort and no one expected it to show when the match began. 'No problem, old boy,' he said cheerfully to O'Connor, who had heard of his condition.

Most of the other players enjoyed a quiet hour with their wives, who regaled them with stories about their coach tour down the coast (the visit to Loch Lomond having been cancelled owing to the weather), visiting some of the lovely fishing villages to be found either side of St Andrews. They had stopped and had lunch at the Craw's Nest Hotel in Anstruther, where the temptation to eat too much is a local hazard and one many were all too happy to face.

The players met at 7 p.m. in the Jacklin Room, and this time their wives were invited to join the gathering. Cotton's wife, Toots, was the star of the show. While her husband told dirty jokes to anyone who listened, Toots moved like a social butterfly from one group of people to another and was the centre of attention wherever she went. The day had improved for Toots. It had started in a rage, for when she left the hotel during the morning to assess the weather and so what to wear for the jaunt to Loch Lomond she saw one or two unfavourable newspaper billboards. Several writers had rather poked fun at Cotton's performance the day before, and in particular his reference to his masseur, and this had been picked up by the circulation managers. Toots saw the billboards and was instantly displeased, and

Nick Faldo. That is one safely in.

Seve Ballesteros. A master from any trap a course can set.

LEFT: Sandy Lyle and Bernhard Langer. A problem shared . . .

RIGHT: Jose-Maria Olazabal. Reading the line.

LEFT: Henry Cotton. Ever stylish.
BELOW: Christy O'Connor. Known as 'Himself'.

ABOVE: Eric Brown. Grim
determination and a will to win.
RIGHT: Brian Barnes. Toughness
beneath a calm exterior.

ABOVE: Bernard Gallagher. Choosing the right club.
OPPOSITE: Nick Faldo and Peter Oosterhuis. Tee discussion.

LEFT: Ian Woosnam. The little man winds up.

BELOW: Olazabal and Ballesteros. Inseparable (*Phil Sheldon Golf Picture Library*).

OPPOSITE: Jack Nicklaus and Tom Watson. Players and clubs undercover.

LEFT: Sam Snead. A master craftsman.
OPPOSITE: Byron Nelson. Graceful and thoughtful on the course.

RIGHT: Gene Sarazen. Compact player, sweet swing.

RIGHT: Arnold Palmer. Great
technique but able to
adapt it.
BELOW: Billy Casper.
Dependable and consistent.

LEFT: Lee Trevino. With a smile and a wisecrack.
BELOW: Tony Lema. 'Champagne' Tony, loved by the crowds.

ABOVE: Tony Jacklin, non-playing Captain of the
European team, with Lee Trevino.
OPPOSITE: Tom Kite. Striving for perfection.

Walter Hagen, non-playing Captain of the USA team
(*Dave Shatford/Ben Clingain*).

Snead, Sarazen and Nelson. Gentlemen all (*Phil Sheldon
Golf Picture Library*).

decided there and then to do something about it. With her bare
hands she tore them down and when finally someone asked her
what on earth she thought she was doing, she replied: 'But they've
been perfectly beastly to Henry!'

Cotton was not to be totally upstaged at this evening show.
When the waiter entered the room to start to serve the four-course
meal he found every guest down on their knees with Cotton asking
the Lord to deal kindly with them in the morning and to ask the
Goddess of Luck to smile favourably on them during the course of
the next three days. Several members of the party looked bemused
by this proposition from a man whom no one would have
considered a religious fanatic. The Langers, though, thought it a
lovely gesture, and Cotton was at least content in the knowledge
that while he could not be sure the Lord himself was listening, at
least he would have one of his keenest followers by his side come
the afternoon fourballs. Surely he would not let any bad luck
befall Bernhard, Cotton thought to himself.

Barnes was in terrific spirits as well. He had decided to limit his
intake of beer on this, the eve of the match, and he'd all but
reached his unwonted target with the night still young. He was
teasing Eric Brown. 'Did you see Sarazen's face on Tuesday night
when you told him he couldn't hold a candle any more to Nick
Faldo? Eric, you sure know how to make yourself popular with
the Americans, don't you? We could do with you on the first tee in
the morning to have a go at Nicklaus and Hogan and upset them
before we tee off.'

At 9 p.m. the gathering split up but before the players returned
to their rooms, Jacklin had one final thing to say: 'Gentlemen,
we've had a lot of hype and a lot of speculation but I just want you
to know that I'm proud that you've all qualified for the team and
I'm proud of the spirit we have going here.

'And I think it's important that we remember to enjoy ourselves
out there. Don't get too screwed up, or too tight. And don't have a
sleepless night. I'll see most of you in the morning at 6.30 a.m.'

―――――――――――

After the opening ceremony, Hagen had agreed to have an early
evening drink with journalists from some of the leading dailies in
America. These writers were lucky in that they had far more

relaxed deadlines. It was 6 p.m. when they met but as far as work was concerned only 1 p.m. for the *New York Times*, 12 noon for the *Chicago Tribune*, while the sports editor of the *Los Angeles Times* had still to reach his office.

The writers caught Hagen at a good moment. He was in expansive mood. He felt he had nothing to keep back any more. He admitted that he hoped that Hogan would be fit enough to play in all matches. 'What was Hogan's reaction?', added a reporter.

'Oh, we sat and talked it through for a couple of hours,' Hagen said, as the journalists laughed.

'How on earth could you not play Arnie?'

'Thirty is not his age any more. That's how long he's been playing top-class golf. I still think Palmer will make a valuable contribution to this team but I don't think he would if he was playing in every match.'

'Have you managed to calm Sam down?'

'Sure, he's fine. Apart from the food, the golf course, the service, the facilities, losing money on the first two days and probably my captaincy, I don't think he's upset about anything.'

'What's your opinion about Eric Brown?'

'I may be wrong but I suspect Eric is just an act. He needs to wind himself up like MacEnroe. If he believes he hates the opposition then he's as good as anybody. He needs to have a cause. I may be wrong. He may have a pathological hatred of all players who come from the other side of the Atlantic. But I suspect that if you met Eric during the middle of the season, he would be the first to come over and let you buy him a drink.'

'Would you like to see a singles match between Eric and Sam?'

'I'd sure like to see it watching through my fingers. That would be quite something, wouldn't it? It's just too horrible to contemplate. It would probably end the special relationship between Britain and America there and then.'

'Do you think Jacklin did any point scoring at the opening ceremony?'

'How do you mean? With his little bit about saying how many Ryder Cups his players have competed in? Nah. I think if our players are fazed by that they may as well give up.'

The writers asked what he was going to be doing after the Ryder Cup. Hagen said he was going to play in the BMW International in

Germany the following week, if only for the fact that a brand new top-of-the-range example of the sponsor's wares would appear on his drive a couple of weeks later. He would be spending the winter making a movie. It was a thriller, he said. He'd read the plot not long before coming away, and he just hoped that the Ryder Cup proved equally suspenseful.

The conversation continued for an hour. Hagen had just a couple of Scotches before telling the writers that he would have to rejoin his team. He was still in his Ralph Lauren blazer when he entered the Hagen Room, where everyone else had changed and was now in casual clothes. 'Go straight to the bar?', Lema enquired.

Hagen didn't reply. Instead he made the waiter go round everybody to get their dinner orders and then he made sure that every player sat next to a player's wife so long as it was not his own. 'For a couple of hours, we're not going to talk golf,' he said.

They didn't either. Unless you count Barbara Nicklaus talking to Arnold Palmer about Japan, and how Jack was off there after the Ryder Cup to play in a couple of tournaments.

Claudia Trevino talked to the captain about his Hollywood life and wanted to know what so-and-so was really like, just as millions of other people have wanted to know what her husband was really like.

In truth Lee Trevino was not that comfortable in this kind of situation. There were moments in every day when the man considered the arch-joker just wanted to be alone, and he often spent evenings in his room watching television and ordering room service. He was sitting next to Tom Kite's wife, Christy, but the pair didn't share many words, and Trevino was glad when the hour was over and he could talk to the man who was sitting almost opposite, Lloyd Mangrum. Trevino wanted to ask him about Eric Brown – and what American didn't want to talk about Brown? – because he had a sneaky feeling that he would be playing him come the following afternoon. 'He's a nasty ba . . .,' Mangrum said, stopping himself from swearing on account of the company present. Mangrum had a habit of talking out of the corner of his mouth and it made everything he said sound as though he were relating a conspiracy theory. 'He pulled me up on the tee once. Accused me of gamesmanship. That was on the 17th. I was still shaking with anger when he beat me on the last. If you play him, Lee, beat him. Beat him good. But I want to play him in the singles.'

Hagen had set a 9.30 p.m. curfew for his team and as that time approached he stood on his feet and gave his team his goodnight message. 'Well, fellas,' he said, 'I like what I see. I think we've got the perfect blend of working hard and yet doing it with a smile. It's going to be a tough three days, we can be sure of that. But there's no question that we are the better players and we have to make that count. I'm very pleased with you all. Your attitude has been spot on and you've all been very helpful. I really couldn't have asked for more at this stage. So as they say in Hollywood: lights, cameras, action!'

5

Friday:
The Contest Begins

FROM OUT OF the darkness they came; so many headlights, snaking along the highways leading to St Andrews. From above the whole scene must have resembled those moments at a rock concert when the lights go out and the audience hold up lit torches in recognition of the fact that the band has played the first bars of its signature tune.

But this was 6.30 in the morning and only on days like the one about to unfold did you see cluttered roads in this or indeed any part of Fife. In the next hour these true golfing people would be parked, they would have breakfasted on bacon rolls, and they would be standing or sitting somewhere along the first hole, waiting for the initial shots to be fired in the Ryder Cup.

Hogan was due to hit the first ball at 8 a.m. but long before that there wasn't a spare seat or place to be found anywhere that afforded a view of that opening hole. The 'Stands Full' signs were up by the time first light had stolen through. Behind the ropes, where the foot soldiers prepared to take their long march out and then back again, they stood six deep, with Ryder Cup periscopes in hand in an effort to gain the merest glimpses of the action.

St Andrews was waking up to find itself suffocating with people. In the newsagents' they queued to buy their daily read to see if anything sensational had occurred overnight. The restaurants near the course that had decided to break the habit of a lifetime and open to serve breakfast were well rewarded for their efforts.

Even the media tent was at least half full as journalists put on their armbands and prepared to walk a few holes in their enviable avenues inside the ropes.

There was no sign of Hogan or Nicklaus, or Barnes or Gallacher. They were all still on the practice ground. Hogan had now entered his concentration zone and was saying little. Barnes had entered his as well and accordingly was rabbiting away to anyone who listened.

Hogan was undergoing his now time-honoured routine. He expected to hit a driver off the 1st tee and a wedge into the 2nd green and so he practised with those two clubs for a time. Then he turned back to the driver he would use off the 3rd tee and the long iron he would need to the 4th green. Would it be a 2 iron? Or a 3? Or with Nicklaus, maybe even a 4. Hogan hit twenty shots with each just to make sure. Nothing was ever left to something as whimsical as chance.

The sky was overcast but it was not cold and the Americans wore just one red cashmere sweater each over their pristine white polo necks. The two Scots both felt they needed only a sweater and a polo shirt. The colour of the day for the Europeans was brown: brown trousers, brown polo shirt, brown sweater, all of them different shades. Very autumnal.

The practice ground at St Andrews is situated at the far end of the Old Course and necessitates transport to get back to the first tee. Even on the practice ground there wasn't a spare seat to be had. The small grandstand behind where the players warmed up was, despite the earliness of the hour, already filled to capacity.

The players were politely informed that they would have to move to the 1st tee in five minutes. Nicklaus and Hogan looked at each other but said nothing. Both Jacklin and Hagen looked far more relaxed than any of the players. With thirty minutes to tee-off time they stepped into the cars that would escort them around to the 1st tee.

It was perhaps as well that all four players were experienced campaigners because the most daunting scene greeted them. Later Barnes would say: 'Everywhere you looked there were people. They were hanging out of windows and standing on tiptoe just straining for a peek. It was nerve-racking in one sense but very inspiring as well. It filled you with a warm glow.'

The cars pulled up at the entrance to the clubhouse to rapturous acclaim. All four players sought refuge for a few minutes in the shelter of the locker room, where they were alone and could fill their minds with the task ahead.

When they emerged there was just fifteen minutes to go. They made their way to the small makeshift practice putting green next to the 1st tee. Barnes strolled over to the galleries and signed one or two autographs. The clock next to the tee appeared to be ticking over in slow motion. Jacklin had a chat with Gallacher, who would strike the first blow for Europe.

And then came the announcement that everyone had been waiting for. 'Good morning, ladies and gentlemen, and welcome to the Ryder Cup. In this opening match, for the Americans, Jack Nicklaus and Ben Hogan.' The applause rang out from all areas around the opening hole. It was warm and it was affectionate but, Jacklin noted to himself, it lacked passion. 'For Europe, Bernard Gallacher and Brian Barnes.' It didn't lack passion now. 'The Americans will tee off first. On the tee, Ben Hogan.'

Barnes, Gallagher v. Hogan, Nicklaus
There were times in Hogan's life when he couldn't have handled a situation like this. All those people. All that mental turmoil. Now he placed his ball on the tee, and stared out at the vast acreage of safe ground ahead. A couple of trademark waggles and then a perfect Hogan swing, just like on the practice ground, just like during all those tournament victories. He had aimed just left of the centre ground and the ball pierced the air on its intended flight path and came to rest some 260 yards from the tee. 'Perfect,' said Nicklaus to his partner.

Hogan had always believed that the drive is the most important shot in golf. It sets up everything else and everything comes from it. For Gallacher's sake it was just as well that there was more than one way to play the game. Driving had never been his forte. Guts, yes, chipping, yes, putting, yes, driving, no. No applause greeted his effort. It barely got off the ground. For one awful moment it looked as though he had topped the ball. In the event it somehow clawed its way to the 200-yard mark. 'Fine, Bernie,' Barnes said.

And so they were on their way and the crowd roared after them as they began their journey down the game's most historic fairway. For the four players concerned this was the one moment when their hopes and fears were the same, before fate took hold of them and escorted them down wildly contrasting roads.

Perhaps it was the hour, Nicklaus thought, or perhaps this was how the weather would be throughout the first day. Whatever, there was only the slightest breeze as they strolled down the 1st fairway after their tee shots. If it stayed like this all morning it would be against the players on the front nine and helping them on the way home.

It didn't take Barnes many of his enormous strides to reach Gallacher's ball. On a hole where normally he would be thinking of a wedge or, at most, a 9 iron, he was now torn between a hard 8 or a smooth 7. Gallacher thought he should hit the 7. His thinking was clear: the last thing they wanted to do was to finish in the Swilcan Burn at the front of the green. To lose the first hole to a par would be a sin on a day such as this and a terrible start to the event.

Barnes chose a 7. It was indeed a smooth swing. The flag had been cut 10 ft on to the green. Barnes's shot was slightly right of the flag and long. He was 30 ft from the pin.

Nicklaus had already decided that he was going to hit a wedge by the time Barnes's ball was in flight. It pitched 20 ft past the flag and came to a dead stop a yard or so later. Clearly, the strategy of both teams on this opening hole was safety first.

Neither birdie putt threatened the hole and only Barnes was required to tap home from 2 ft to halve the 1st in pars. Nicklaus drove off from the 2nd to a mighty round of applause but once more the Scottish drive was not what had been hoped for. It was left, too far left as it turned out, and it finished in Cheape's Bunker. Gallacher could do nothing else but pitch it out, 30 yards further down the fairway. With its ridges and hollows the 2nd hole is not one where it is easy to get the ball close to the hole, even with a wedge in one's hands. As things now stood, of course, there was no need for Hogan to try and he was quietly satisfied as his approach finished 20 ft from the flag. Barnes's wedge shot stopped just inside Hogan's.

Jacklin was watching on a little television monitor that had been installed in the buggy he would have for the week to drive him around the course. He was perched by the 17th tee as both Nicklaus and Gallacher missed their putts. One down. 'Not the start we were looking for,' he said to Rees.

The 3rd hole was halved in pars and so was the 4th but at least here the large contingent of spectators who had decided to follow this match had something to cheer. For after Gallacher had missed the green with his approach, Barnes chipped to 15 ft, and his partner holed to prevent the pair falling 2 behind.

The Americans, though, were hugely impressive. So impressive, in fact, that Hagen decided he had watched enough of this match and dropped back to pick up Watson and Nelson, who had just reached the first green.

At the long 5th Hogan's drive once more split the fairway and when he got up to the ball and saw it lying perfectly, Nicklaus reached for his 3 wood, opened his shoulders and smashed the ball just short of the hollow that fronts the green. The ball rolled up to 40 ft from the flag. There was no hope of Barnes keeping up with such a blow, but Gallacher, from 70 yards short of the green, pitched up to 12 ft.

Hogan's putt finished stone dead for a textbook birdie. Barnes's birdie effort caught the left edge of the hole and fell below ground. More cheers. The Scots were holding on by their shoelaces.

There was little or no conversation between the four players. This had nothing to do with gamesmanship or impoliteness but merely indicated the concentration being expended. Even Barnes was saying little, and all of it directed at his partner.

In anticipation of the hole being slightly into the wind, the pin at the 6th was positioned on the front of the green. Nevertheless, the Americans found a way to get the ball close, as Hogan's approach finished 6 ft from the flag. The Scots were 25 ft away, and Barnes, anticipating what would happen next, duly went for his birdie and knocked the ball 4 ft past. He was right to give it a go. Nicklaus's putt never erred from the middle of the hole.

The Americans went 3 up with a third consecutive birdie at the 7th, and the 2 that the Scots registered at the short 8th proved but a moment's relief when the Americans made a 3 at the 9th to be out in an ominous 32 blows. There were no cheers filtering back down the course from this match, only applause for some imperious golf from the visitors.

Hogan and Nicklaus had not indulged in much conversation in practice before the match. Implicitly, neither felt the need. If this had been a stroke play tournament they would have approached it with this philosophy: play to prevent mistakes for 54 holes and see how we lie. If ever there was a format in golf to which this game plan was even more perfectly suited then it was surely foursomes.

On this day, though, the Americans were doing so much better than merely avoiding mistakes. Over the opening nine they hadn't been in trouble off any drive and hadn't come remotely close to missing any green in regulation. The Scots had made just one mistake and found themselves trailing by an extremely daunting margin.

It didn't widen over the next three holes but neither did it narrow. The Americans made pars and invited the Scots to try for birdies to close the gap. Barnes had outside chances at the 10th and again at the 12th but both putts stubbornly refused to drop.

The 13th was halved in pars as well and then at the long 14th they finally got a break, when Nicklaus misjudged his pitch shot to the green. The ball landed on the top of the rise that signals the start of the putting surface but then started to spin back down the slope. Hogan was left with a putt of only 35 ft but now he had to come up the sharp bank and his effort went 8 ft past. Gallacher, from wide of the flag to the left, putted up to a length such that Hogan had no hesitation in conceding the putt for par. Now for the first time there was a moment of pressure on the Americans, the first time they had flirted with taking a bogey. Nicklaus's putt was never hard enough. It lost its line 6 inches from the hole and dribbled past the right edge. The cheer was a loud one but Nicklaus was sensible enough to know they were applauding a European success and not his mistake. It was enough to send Jacklin hurtling across the course in his buggy.

The Americans were now 2 up, which was hardly a just reflection on the quality of ball striking that had been going on. If justice had been served they would by now have been preparing to be driven in to contemplate their afternoon exertions and reflect on a morning victory. But when has golf been a fair game? Gallacher kept the pressure on with a perfect drive.

There are times in every match when the moment arrives which determines in which direction the wheel is going to spin. For all their splendid golf, the Americans subconsciously knew they had now reached that moment. Lose another hole and with the 17th to come anything really could happen. The spectators were making their own calculations: if the Europeans could just somehow get something from this match then what an invaluable bonus that would prove and what an inspiring effect it could have on their colleagues playing behind!

The two people, though, who had none of these thoughts at the front of their minds were Nicklaus and Hogan. Get one step ahead of yourself in golf and that's the path to ruin, and no one avoided that temptation better than these two. Hogan's drive finished 20 yards ahead, on the same line as Gallacher's.

Barnes's iron shot was an excellent one in the circumstances. It finished 14 ft from the flag. The response from Nicklaus, though, was truly golden. The ball grazed the flagstick and finished 2 ft away. Gallacher, for all his grim determination, could not coax his putt into the hole. Hogan had no problems with his short one.

The moment therefore had come and gone and the Americans had survived. Ten minutes later, they had won the first point of the match, as the 16th was halved in par 4s to give the visitors a 3 and 2 victory. They had gone round in 3 under par and while their play on the back nine had hardly matched the sparkle of the outward half, the feeling persisted that it hadn't done so simply because the circumstances hadn't warranted such a response. The one time they were truly threatened they had produced a most magical solution. It was clear they inspired one another and when one came up with a special shot the other felt a keen need to follow it with something similar.

Hagen came rushing on to the green and gave each an exuberant greeting, with one arm round the shoulders and the other warmly shaking the hand. He shook hands with the losers too, and Barnes said: 'There was nothing we could do on the day.' He repeated his words to Jacklin, although the European captain knew well enough.

The players retreated to the waiting buggies. Hogan and Nicklaus headed back in the direction of the hotel, for they knew that more of the same would be required after lunch. Barnes and Gallacher were going back out on to the course. Their services would be required no more until the morning at the earliest.

Faldo, Oosterhuis v. Nelson, Watson

Nelson was the first American to reach the Hagen Room for breakfast. He managed some cereal before heading out for the practice ground but he couldn't have hit more than forty shots before leaving there and hurriedly exiting in the direction of the hotel. Nelson was feeling nauseous, and duly vomited with one hour to go before his tee-off time. 'That's better,' he said to himself.

It was often this way. Nelson found it hard to retain food before a big occasion and had come to look upon it as a positive sign. Nevertheless, thoughts of retirement flooded his head even though he was still a relatively young man. He thought of the ranch back home in Texas. He thought of his haemophilia. 'You look pale, partner,' Watson said to him as Nelson reached the practice ground for a second time.

'So would you in my shoes,' Nelson replied. He wondered whether he would throw up again before he teed off but this thought soon passed as he settled into his practice routine. Like so many great players Nelson possessed an assiduous work ethic. His exaggerated leg action had been tempered as he had got older but he still felt the need to work on his game morning, noon and night to compensate for a putting stroke that at its best was very good but at times could be extremely brittle. A bit like Tom Watson's, in fact, although he had never felt, at any stage of his career, as confident as his playing partner had when he was winning all his major titles. Not even when Nelson himself had been winning tournaments with monotonous ease.

Nelson looked up and admired Watson's easy rhythm. Glancing further along he admired too the diligence with which Faldo went about his business, and also his swing, which, like his own, had improved immeasurably as Faldo had matured. Next in line was Oosterhuis, and Nelson could not resist a quiet chuckle to himself: his ungainly method was certainly going to stand out in this match, wasn't it?

Not that the American would underestimate him. On the contrary, he was genuinely full of admiration that a man could make such a limited action go so far. And he knew that Oosterhuis revelled in just the circumstances with which he was about to be presented. The man who stood 6 ft 5 in tall liked nothing better than being portrayed as a golfing Lilliputian.

Off the 1st tee it was Oosterhuis and Nelson who got matters under way. No problems there. None either with two excellent second shots, but neither putt was holed.

The Americans drew first blood again at the 2nd, only this time with a birdie when Watson holed from 15 ft. The Europeans replied instantly with a birdie of their own at the 3rd, when Faldo's splendid short iron approach gave Oosterhuis an opportunity from 4 ft that proved irresistible.

Both sides bogeyed the long 4th. The Americans 3-putted from almost the entire length of the double green. Oosterhuis's raking 2 iron had bounced away to the right into a green-side bunker, from where there was little chance of getting down in two.

Three pars followed. The Americans had chances at both the 7th and the 8th but Nelson didn't make either birdie putt. At the 10th, he could only stand and watch as Faldo demonstrated the art, holing from 10 ft, and finally the Europeans really had something to cheer. By this stage the top match was already looking a foregone conclusion but the acclaim that greeted Faldo's putt left no one in any doubt that rather better news was emanating from the second match.

Europe continued to hang on to their slender lead: through the 11th, where they got down in two fine putts after a rather sloppy tee shot from Oosterhuis had finished nearer the flag on the 7th than the one at which he was aiming; at the 12th, where Watson's bold decision to go with a driver had been rewarded with neither birdie nor eagle; and at the 13th, where both sides got orthodox pars.

Watson again hit an exemplary drive down the 14th which was now downwind to a helpful degree; with a full-blooded wood, he thought Nelson could perhaps make the front of the green. In the event he came up 30 yards short. Again the Americans could not make the advantage tell. Again they halved in par.

Faldo and Oosterhuis were rather taking a leaf out of the Hogan/Nicklaus scrapbook and concentrating on avoiding errors. If the Americans were going to win a hole they would have to do so with a birdie.

The trouble was that by now Nelson and Watson were both playing too well to keep getting nothing better than 4s. At the 15th they narrowly missed a 3. At the 16th they finally earned their reward. This time it was Watson who had the birdie putt from 10 ft. His nerve held. All square.

The two captains joined this match at almost the same time. Jacklin had audibly groaned as he watched Watson hole his putt on the television monitor. Now he was there in person to see Nelson launch a perfect drive. From the tee, to the unsuspecting spectator, it would have looked to be flying miles out of bounds. The American didn't give it a second's thought. It pitched in the middle of the fairway and ran out of breath 2 yards short of the rough on the left-hand side.

Oosterhuis's drive was a good one too, finishing just in the rough some 15 yards further back.

What was now left was what the Ryder Cup was all about. The second shot to the 17th at St Andrews may well carry an element of good fortune about it but it also called for precision shot making.

Faldo walked after his ball with a brisk march and soon his caddie, Fanny Sunesson, was trailing some 30 yards behind despite her level-best efforts to keep up. She wasn't too worried, however. She knew this was one shot that Faldo would want to think long and hard about. 'Two hundred to the front of the green,' she said.

It was circumstances like this for which Faldo had changed his swing. When the situation called for all his powers of logic and rationale and technique and temperament, it was one he relished. He selected a 4 iron and visualized the ball pitching in the hollow at the front of the green and running up 10 yards on to the putting surface. It pitched exactly where he intended but rather disappointingly moved only half the distance he had surmised. Still, the Europeans were in fine shape. 'Great shot,' said Oosty. With his excellent putting stroke to follow, the worst score the Europeans were realistically looking at was a 4.

The enormous crowd that had gathered behind the wall at the 17th were delighted as well. They had felt short-changed when, after standing there for several hours, they had not seen a blow delivered in the top match. Now they were seeing Faldo against Watson, two of the finest players of all time.

Watson duly responded to the demands of the situation. His soft 5 iron pitched in almost exactly the same spot as Faldo's, only here the ball did hop up on to the green before coming to a halt some half a dozen paces shy of the back edge. It was a terribly courageous blow, for it must have crossed Watson's mind that it might topple over on to the road – and what a horrible fleeting moment that must have been. But it didn't, nor did it deserve to; and now the Americans would have an outside chance of a birdie.

From fully 15 yards Oosterhuis putted up to within 3 inches of the hole. For just a second there was the prospect of a 3 and the crowd roared lustily. Jacklin waved the putt on too. Instinctively,

Oosterhuis knew it was going to finish just short. Nelson picked up the ball. Now Watson, from 35 ft, across a green with many subtle nodes. He missed on the left.

One always has a sense of privilege when standing on the 18th tee at St Andrews and firing off a drive with the right side of the clubhouse the target from where the player gazes. How much more this must be so when the double fairway is heavily lined with spectators and behind the white posts the people are scampering where they can, just straining to get a view of you playing golf at the Home of Golf.

Watson's drive possessed just the slightest hint of a draw and came to rest some 15 yards left of where he had intended. But even so, his partner only had 70 yards to go. Faldo's drive went the other way, leaving Oosterhuis a similar distance to travel, on the other side of the fairway. It would need a referee to decide who would play first.

Eventually it was Nelson who got the nod. What a shot he played. Iron Byron's ball pitched no more than 10 ft over the Valley of Sin and came to rest 18 inches from the flag. The roar of acclaim was matched by a sense of disappointment. Not another defeat, surely? Perhaps not. Oosterhuis is an expert at the pitch shot too. His ball finished 6 ft away.

Faldo and Sunesson surveyed the resultant putt for what seemed an age. As Faldo addressed the ball, his hands appeared to be dancing on the putting grip. Could he not get comfortable? In any other player this would have been taken as a sign of nerves and bets taken that the putt would be missed. But Faldo steadied himself before he began the stroke. He aimed the putt at the right centre of the hole and it darted back as he had intended and fell below ground. He clutched his heart in mock relief and acknowledged the warm applause.

Would the Englishmen concede their opponents' putt? When Watson replaced his ball it was clear it was not a 'gimme'. Neither, though, did he miss it, and the Ryder Cup had witnessed its first halved match.

Woosnam, O'Connor v. Kite, Lema

Watching Christy O'Connor and Ian Woosnam in tandem was one of the great golfing pleasures. Here were two of the purest ball strikers and it was clear they revelled in each other's company. They had been the most relaxed players on view before the Ryder Cup began and they shared the odd quip between warm-up shots.

Typically, Lema came over and shook hands with both and wished them luck but not too much. This was certainly going to be the friendliest match of the four. Yet behind the laughter and the jokes, this was also a Ryder Cup in which O'Connor was desperate to do well. His record was not good and while it was true that he had been unlucky on certain occasions to come up against some stout American play, what was also undeniable was that the contest had not seen the best of the Irishman.

This was a new partnership and one for which both O'Connor and Jacklin had high hopes. The pair were similar in so many ways, and Jacklin felt that the Welshman's smooth rhythm would help O'Connor discover his best form.

It was a tough proposition. If O'Connor hadn't as yet done himself justice in the Ryder Cup, then the opposite most certainly applied in the case of Tom Kite. A leaning towards vulnerability when in contention and confronted by the final holes of major championships was to be replaced by a ferocious determination when the same set of circumstances applied in these matches.

The first few holes were predictably even. O'Connor had an outside chance at the 1st and Lema at the 3rd but they stood on the 6th tee all square, after both sides had swapped par figures. The 6th was halved as well, only this time in birdies. At the 7th, Kite hit a marvellous wedge shot adjacent to the pin to put the Americans 1 hole ahead.

The visitors increased their lead at the 9th when Kite's approach shot again finished close to the flag. The Americans were out in 33, but the Irish–Welsh combination got back in the match with a birdie of their own at the 10th. The home pair felt fortunate to escape with a half at the 11th, after O'Connor's tee shot finished in Strath Bunker. Lema, uncharacteristically, followed him in. The 12th featured some wonderfully adventurous golf. Kite, though not a long hitter, was known for being able to compensate with some of the straightest driving the game had seen. A 1 iron for him here. His drive never left the pin until its last bounce just short of the green. But still it finished 20 ft away. Woosnam had thought about taking an iron for safety but saw no point in such a strategy now. His 3 wood shot was a good one and finished just short of the apron of the green.

There wasn't a player in the event who wouldn't expect to get down in 2 from just off the green, and that was true of O'Connor more than most. But the chip with which he was confronted was hardly of the bread-and-butter variety. There were two slopes to negotiate. He worked it out in his head and then played a delicate little wedge that rolled this way and that and then caressed the flag before falling below ground for an eagle 2. It was the stroke of a master. Lema missed, and so now the match was all square.

The next three holes were halved as well, but at the 16th O'Connor missed a 4-ft putt for a par to give the Americans a lead they held through the 17th. At the 18th Woosnam, going for a big drive, almost knocked himself off his feet. The ball travelled over 320 yards but veered off to the left on the second half of its flight to leave O'Connor with 50 yards to negotiate to the flag.

Lema, off Kite's arrow-straight 3 wood shot, pitched up to 15 ft behind the flag, leaving O'Connor with a semblance of a chance of a half. Would he produce another exquisite wedge shot? Instead he chose a 7 iron to run the ball across the Valley of Sin. It looked the perfect shot when he hit it, but a cruel bounce just short of the green took it under the influence of the top shelf of St Andrews' most famous slope. This had the effect of diverting the ball to the right of where O'Connor had intended. He looked at the ball in disbelief as it finished 20 ft away.

Woosnam now had to hole to keep alive Europe's hopes. He aimed for the top left of the cup but the ball never deviated. He looked at the heavens in horror when it grazed the top edge of the hole but stayed out.

Good fortune had not been with the Europeans so far and particularly not in this match. O'Connor and Woosnam had played well and gelled well. They were round in 69 shots and would hope to win most matches with such a score. But the Americans were now up by 2 points and all eyes turned to the last match to see if the Europeans could avoid a bleak first morning.

Ballesteros, Olazabal v. Mangrum, Snead

Ballesteros couldn't help himself. He just had to stare. For about ten minutes he watched as Snead went through his practice drills. Indeed, it was more a masterclass as Snead revealed the most sublime swing the game has known.

'Imagine being born with a swing like that!', one spectator said admiringly. Snead heard the remark. He turned around and grimaced. He hated people saying things like that. On numerous occasions he had replied: 'You honestly think I was born with this swing? No, I have this swing because I work my butt off. This is no God-given swing.' On this occasion he let it pass.

It may have been just the final match of the opening series of foursomes but clearly a great deal was already riding on it. It was in anticipation that such a thing could happen that both captains had placed such strong pairings in the anchor role.

In statistical terms they were the most successful partnerships of all time. The pairing of Ballesteros and Olazabal, in particular, had everyone in raptures. Who could forget the first morning that they had ever teamed up together, when Olazabal hit the ball sideways and Ballesteros saved him with a series of quite extraordinary recovery shots? Each time he put his arm around the young Spaniard's shoulder, as if to say: 'Don't worry. It's always like this the first time. You'll get the hang of it.' By the end of that Ryder Cup it had been Olazabal saving Ballesteros, but now Europe would almost certainly require an equal helping of magic from both if the redoubtable Snead–Mangrum partnership was to fail.

It was a slow match. With four holes to play they knew all that had happened ahead, and so Ballesteros and Olazabal were aware that only victory would prevent significant daylight appearing between the teams.

So far so good. The Spaniards were 1 hole ahead. They had been 2 down as early as the 5th and at one point Europe trailed in all four matches. They were still 1 down at the turn and had reached the half-way stage in 36 shots, which was decidedly indifferent on such a golf-friendly day as this.

But a rare 2 at the 11th, where Olazabal had holed from 25 ft, was followed by a birdie 4 at the 14th, where Ballesteros had holed from a similar distance. Snead didn't look too impressed and appeared to mutter the words 'Lucky son of a bitch' under his breath. At the 15th Ballesteros drove off first and split the fairway. He tended to look away when Snead was about to drive for fear of being caught in thrall. Snead pierced the fairway as well. The approach shots from Mangrum and Olazabal both safely found the green. Mangrum lit a cigarette. It must have been his thirtieth of the round and they were coming thick and fast now.

Snead's birdie putt never looked like going in. It would have been hilarious to have seen his reaction if Ballesteros had holed from 28 ft but the ball finished 6 inches short. The Spaniard gave an anguished look and jabbered away to his caddy: 'I thought that putt would have been quicker than that. Didn't you think that putt would have been quicker? It was dead on line as well.'

The 16th was halved in pars too. At the 17th Ballesteros pulled his drive but the ball stopped short of the heavy rough, which would have left Olazabal with little chance of making the green in 2. He grimaced as Snead launched an outrageous reply, far, far right of Ballesteros's line. Snead was spot on. The ball finished miles down the hole and in the middle of the fairway. The Americans were certainly in the driving seat.

When Olazabal got up to his ball several of his team-mates had joined Jacklin in offering moral support. Jacklin was talking to Sam Torrance, who had been faithfully following the games and talking to the journalists who were out on the course.

The two Spaniards were soon in consultation as to what Olazabal should do next. He had 198 yards to the front of the green, and a further 20 to the flag. He elected to hit a 4 iron. What he was proposing was an immensely brave shot. He wanted to start the ball out towards the right of the green and then draw it back towards the flag. It was a gamble partly prompted by the fact that Snead had hit his drive so far that Mangrum could well need only a 7 iron for his shot.

Yet like most gambles it could quite easily go wrong. Draw the ball too quickly and Ballesteros would be playing from the Road Hole Bunker. Misjudge it the other way and the ball would finish on the road. Olazabal had fully half a dozen practice swings before he felt sure in his own mind of what he was about to do.

He watched the flight of the ball very carefully. It pitched 10 yards short of the hollow and from there it started to take the spin. Yes . . . up the slope now . . . keep going . . . keep going . . . settle down now . . . settle down. The ball finished 18 ft from the flag. It was the shot of the morning.

Mangrum did indeed hit a 7 iron but he left Snead with little chance of making a birdie. The resultant 30-ft putt travelled 6 ft past, but Mangrum was not to get the opportunity to try to hole. Ballesteros liked the look of the putt from the moment he first started to assess the line, and he liked the idea of putting the perfect gloss on a shot from Olazabal that he would later describe as one of the best he had seen all year. Ballesteros holed for a 2 and 1 victory. Olazabal ran over to him and the pair embraced warmly. They shook hands with the vanquished and Snead's disappointment was visible for all to see. The two captains respectively congratulated and commiserated with each other.

———————

At the press conference afterwards Jacklin spoke of his relief at the final match going their way. 'The Americans are just so strong that I don't know if there would have been any way back for our guys if we had finished the morning trailing by 3 points.

'Seve and Ollie saved the day. That point was vital and will give us tremendous heart. To trail by 1 point at this stage is nothing, and fourballs is always our strongest game. I don't know why we don't seem to do that well in foursomes but we don't.'

Hagen said: 'I'm delighted with our morning's work. I thought Jack and Ben did a great job this morning. It was important to us that Brian and Bernard didn't get off to a fast start and lift the crowd, and our pair ensured that wasn't the case by playing magnificent golf over that front nine.

'I'm delighted with Tom and Tony as well. I think they're going to surprise a lot of people this week. Tom's just such a great Ryder Cup player. I think the last match could well have gone either way but we just saw a bit of that Spanish genius at the end. That was a helluva shot of José's.'

The two captains, as required by the rules of the competition, had submitted their fourballs pairings some ninety minutes earlier. This was how it had worked out:

> Brown, Lyle v. Palmer, Sarazen
> Woosnam, O'Connor v. Nicklaus, Hogan
> Cotton, Langer v. Trevino, Casper
> Ballesteros, Olazabal v. Mangrum, Snead

The captains had seen the draw earlier but hadn't really studied it. Now they had a moment to digest the information. They were asked for their thoughts.

Hagen said: 'The bottom match should be interesting! I think those four will enjoy playing each other again. There's four hard competitors there.'

Jacklin said: 'I think it is important that we get off to a better start in the fourballs. We can't afford to be trailing in all four matches early on as we were this morning.'

In the information trays in the media tent were a few one-sentence quotes from the players. Barnes said: 'We ran into a steamroller.'

Hogan said: 'Nothing to say right now.'

Woosnam commented: 'We're delighted with the way we played and if we keep going like that we'll pick up some points. We're playing against Nicklaus and Hogan this afternoon? You've got to be joking.'

The players had little time to contemplate the morning's play. Just twenty-five minutes stood between the last shot played by Ballesteros and the first that would be played after lunch by Palmer. As Ballesteros was finishing a quick sandwich he watched on television as Palmer was given an affectionate round of applause when he stepped on to the 1st tee.

Brown, Lyle v. Palmer, Sarazen

Protocol demanded that Eric Brown shake hands with his two opponents before teeing off but that was about the extent of his greeting. He felt no desire to embroider this custom by offering words of good luck or some such phraseology, simply because the last thing he wanted was for the Americans to enjoy any fortune.

And so it was that the Brown mask was in place and his face was set hard against Palmer and Sarazen. In an idle moment Nicklaus once referred to the Ryder Cup as a war, without really meaning it. But for Brown this was the equivalent of going into battle for his country.

He had heard that his name had often cropped up in American conversation, and examples of past abruptness had been oft quoted. It was music to his ears. 'Any time the opposition are talking about you must be a good thing,' he said to himself. He just hoped big Sandy was up to the task as well. He could be brilliant, of that there was no doubt, but the head quickly dropped if things were not right. 'Not today,' Brown thought to himself. 'Whatever happens.'

Lyle dumped his second shot in the burn at the 1st. He looked across at Brown and mouthed an apology. Brown hit his approach to 30 ft but couldn't match Palmer's birdie to start.

Palmer had been itching all morning to play. He thought he would enjoy watching the morning razzmatazz blow itself out before going out to play but as he stepped on to a deserted practice ground at 11 a.m. he found he missed it. 'Damn, those three shots felt good,' he said to himself as he made the short walk from the opening green to the 2nd tee.

Brown cut across Lyle's walk as he made the same journey. Lyle wondered what he had done wrong now. Surely he was not going to get a rollicking for what happened at the very first hole? Brown said: 'No apologies, laddy, OK? I'll presume you're trying your damnedest. I know you won't want to let me down.'

The last sentence was delivered with a fair bit of menace. Or so Lyle thought. Anyway, he did try his damnedest and it was good enough. Lyle birdied no fewer than six of the next nine holes and Brown chipped in with a birdie of his own to make the Europeans 7 under par during that spell.

Several of the birdies were cancelled out by the Americans. But not the ones at the 2nd, the 4th, the 7th and the 10th. Europe were 3 up playing the 11th. The crowd were loving this. The two Scots were much loved, and not just because of their nationality. Brown's hard-as-nails approach inspired much affection, as did his refusal to be daunted. Yet Lyle commanded equal reverence, because here was a player who was the equal of practically anyone in terms of natural ability.

The pin at the 11th had been cut just over the Strath Bunker and neither Lyle nor Brown could get too close to it. Palmer decided to dabble with the bunker. If this had been a stroke play situation he would have struck a 6 iron but this was a throwback to the Palmer of yore. He took a 7, and the ball pitched a yard over the bunker and rolled on down to the flag. Sarazen applauded. Brown didn't.

The Scots were still 2 ahead standing on the 14th tee, when Brown had a quiet word with Lyle. 'You're on fire, Sandy. You're just about the only player in the field who can reach this bugger in 2. Give it your best shot.' Off a perfect drive, Lyle hooked his second stroke with a 3 wood but such is his length he still found himself on the green. That was the good news. The bad was that he was fully 140 ft from the pin. 'Maybe I should take a driver,' he said to his caddy. 'Maybe you should get down in 2,' he replied. 'Eric thinks this is the crucial moment in the match.'

It was. None of the other three looked like getting a birdie. Lyle was often described as an indifferent putter and there were days when he didn't appear to have any feel on the greens. But in general he possessed an excellent touch and never more so than when standing over a putt such as this. It was one of Lyle's good days. And accordingly, the ball swooped and soared over the humps and hollows and came to rest 8 ft from the flag. Even Brown felt like applauding that one. Lyle holed it.

Three up with four to play against Palmer and Sarazen. A notable scalp was now within reach for the Europeans. A point that would tie the score overall. Perhaps Lyle and Brown were thinking too much of this because both managed to get bogey 5s down the rather easy par 4 15th. Then again, perhaps it was the jolt they needed. Under the watching eye of Jacklin, Brown closed out the match with a birdie at the 16th. The Scots were 8 under par to that point and even though fourballs golf encourages spectacular scoring, it was still some going.

Both Sarazen and Palmer found it hard to offer anything other than cursory handshakes to Brown at the end although they were generous in their praise of Lyle. They knew they had played well enough and that the big Scot had enjoyed one of those days when he would have beaten anybody. Jacklin was exuberant. 'Brilliant, Sandy, just brilliant. I told you playing with Eric wouldn't be that awful.'

'You know the bad news about this, Sandy, don't you?', Brown said to his partner. Lyle was thinking: 'Is there any pleasing this man? I've just gone round in about 65 and he's still complaining.'

'No, what?', said Lyle. Brown broke out into a broad grin.

'It means you've got me again tomorrow.'

Woosnam, O'Connor v. Nicklaus, Hogan

'Whatever happened to the luck of the Irish?', Woosnam had said to his partner over their quick sandwich at lunchtime.

'Cancelled out by my bad luck in the Ryder Cup,' O'Connor replied. It was certainly tough on the European pair, having played so well in the morning only to lose, to find themselves confronted by arguably the strongest pairing in the tournament.

Woosnam had asked Barnes during the interval whether the

Americans had been that good in the morning or whether the Scots had struggled. 'Do you want me to lie and say we played badly and handed it to them, or do you want the truth?', Barnes answered.

Yet by the time 1.15 p.m. came around and they were on the tee, both Woosnam and O'Connor had worked themselves up into the right condition to play their intimidating opponents. When Woosnam is on form he relishes such combat. And he knew that in O'Connor he had a partner who wouldn't flinch at the prospect of playing two supreme golfers. 'Remember two things,' Jacklin said to them before they were due to tee off. 'No one in this game is unbeatable. And Jack has got a crap record in the Ryder Cup.'

The 1st hole was playing a lot easier that afternoon. The slight breeze against helped the players with their approach shots. There were fewer nerves to contend with as well. They were now into the flow of the competition. O'Connor's approach finished 5 ft away and he holed the putt. Hogan's finished closer and he holed as well. So, it was going to be that sort of match, was it?

It was. Woosnam birdied the 2nd but Hogan birdied the 3rd. Woosnam birdied the 5th but so did Nicklaus. Hogan got a 3 at the 7th but Woosnam levelled the match at the 9th. It was captivating stuff from two pairs of players who could hardly have adopted two more radically different approaches. There were Woosnam and O'Connor, consulting over virtually every shot, often at length, and talking incessantly between shots and on the tee. There were Hogan and Nicklaus, who probably exchanged around a hundred words on the front nine.

And here, too, was the glory of golf and its fascination, its ability to appeal to players of all shapes and sizes and every sort of personality. The game has no prejudice in this respect, unlike any other major sport one cares to mention. Truly, it is sport for all.

The 10th and the 11th were halved in pars, but at the 12th a birdie from the Americans proved decisive. It was Hogan rather than Nicklaus who found the green with his drive.

At the 14th Nicklaus drove into the Elysian Fields, a magnificent blow. Woosnam's drive finished in the Beardies, and so he was effectively out of the hole. O'Connor's sweet swing didn't falter. He followed Nicklaus's line, falling just 15 yards behind the Golden Bear. Hogan was straight as well, and played his second shot first. He cleared Hell Bunker but couldn't make the green. Nor could O'Connor. Nicklaus had 260 yards left, which made the shot at the outer limit of his range with a 3 wood. He hit it nevertheless. With Hogan in fine shape it would have been foolish not to have tried. It was a free shot, in effect, and not only was Nicklaus the best player in the world under pressure, but he was pretty good under these circumstances as well.

The ball effortlessly cleared the monstrously large bunker situated some 90 yards from the green and skipped and bounded its way on to the putting surface, some 20 ft from the flag. The Europeans were in some difficulty now. They knew they could hardly afford to go 2 down to Nicklaus and Hogan. The situation called therefore for some of the short-game wizardry with which O'Connor had made his name. He obliged. His wedge shot, beautifully played in low, checked on its second bounce and finished 18 inches from the flag. Woosnam shook his hand. O'Connor smiled broadly and touched his visor as the applause rose.

It was a classic match play situation. Hogan's third shot had finished 20 ft away. Nicklaus was 45 ft away in 2. It was a very tricky putt and Nicklaus could quite easily charge it 6 ft past and miss the return. Perhaps it was with this in mind that he surveyed the putt for what seemed an age. Eventually he struck it and with two-thirds of its journey completed it was clear this was not a putt that was going to finish 6 ft past. 'Go in,' coaxed Jack. 'Go in.' Was it running out of steam? Just before the hole there was a small bump and the putt gathered enough momentum as it came off the top of it for it to carry just far enough to toppple over the edge of the cup. 'Yes!', the watching Hagen shouted, breaking off an animated conversation with a young woman in the gallery. Nicklaus held his putter in the air. It was such a good putt that even Hogan came over to exchange a few words.

To say the Europeans were deflated would not be telling the half of it. A wonderful shot from O'Connor had come to nought. Once more they were playing well but gaining no reward. Things didn't change over the next few holes either, and the Americans ran out 2 and 1 victors.

O'Connor fell into the arms of a cluster of waiting Irish journalists and the party consoled each other. 'What can you do?', one of them said to O'Connor. 'I think all you can do is take your hat off to the Americans,' O'Connor said graciously.

Cotton, Langer v. Trevino, Casper

Cotton was not best pleased with Europe's morning performance. He didn't want to enter the fray trailing the Americans already by a point. He was certain that he and Langer would not have been beaten at a format to which he felt they were perfectly suited.

He watched a bit of the morning play on television but found it impossible to get involved. He struck a few balls on the range but his concentration was disturbed. He went back to his room and fidgeted until 11.30 a.m., when it was time to begin the routine that he always adopted before playing.

Langer was a much more relaxed soul. He did some exercise to aid his chronic back condition and then had a massage before doing some practice. Trevino and Casper were already on the range.

When he was away from a golf tournament Trevino would quite happily reach a practice ground at 9 a.m. He would hit balls for three hours and then have a sandwich that had been made for him earlier. After that he would hit some more balls and then go back to his buggy where he would have an afternoon nap. On waking he would hit some more balls before packing up for the day. When he was at a tournament, though, he would hit only enough balls to warm up.

His warm-up finished, he indulged in some banter with his caddie, Herman, and a small gathering of people in the stand. 'Play well, Lee,' someone said. 'Aw, come on now, you don't mean that,' Trevino said.

He didn't really play well by his standards either. Casper was principally responsible for the Americans still being in this match over the outward half. He had three birdies, which cancelled out a similar number from Cotton, but Langer had a couple and so Europe were 2 up after nine holes.

Trevino finally managed a birdie at the 10th but Cotton followed him in from 6 ft. Cotton was playing superbly. He was giving a ruthless demonstration of the accuracy from tee to green which had always been his trademark. Apart from Brown and perhaps Ballesteros, no one more enjoyed the opportunity of beating an American than Cotton. His fifth birdie in twelve holes put Europe 3 up at that stage.

Jacklin and Rees had now come over to lend their support. 'Do you think Henry is trying to prove me wrong about this morning?', Jacklin said, smiling at his vice-captain.

Trevino wasn't smiling any more. After his putt lipped out at the 13th he threw his putter to the ground. A rare hooked drive into the Beardies at the 14th saw him swearing to himself all the way down the fairway. Cotton birdied that one too. This was turning into something of a rout for the Europeans.

Casper, dour and professional, was determined to stick to his game plan of playing the course and not his opponents, even given the parlous circumstances. To say this annoyed Trevino was putting it mildly. 'Why is he not having a go?', he said to Hagen at one point.

'You know Billy,' Hagen replied. Nevertheless, cautious approach or not, it was Casper who birdied the 15th and the 16th to give the Americans a semblance of a chance.

Casper's putting method was hardly one that could be recommended, yet it was one that both Cotton and Langer envied and now there was the fear that he had finally found his range on the greens. Trevino, too, could always be relied upon to produce the unexpected, and the 17th was perfectly made for his fade off the tee.

He duly started the ball much more to the left than any other player but it was a beauty, and by the time it had finished rolling it was in a perfect position, in the left-hand side of the fairway. Casper hit a good one too, and so did Cotton, with that deceptively lazy rhythm of his. Langer let go of his driver with his right hand as soon as he struck the ball, and no wonder, as it sailed into the thick rough on the left, leaving him no chance of reaching the green in 2. The penultimate hole at St Andrews is a good one to be holding a 2-hole lead in a fourballs match. It is a very difficult hole at which to make 3, even when you've got two chances at it. But a couple of goes certainly increases the likelihood of registering a par, and this was what the Europeans set out to do as they marched after their drives. For Langer, though, this had become a stiff target and one he failed to manage. But Cotton's approach found the safe part of the green, and now the Americans would need something out of the ordinary.

For a while it looked as if Trevino might deliver. If the drive was perfect for his shape, then the second shot could not be more unhelpful. Nevertheless he tried a low running shot that looked for a long time as if it might finish close. Ultimately, he had misjudged it by the barest amount and he became the first player in this Ryder Cup to finish on the road. Casper's approach was disappointing. It finished outside Cotton's and gave him little chance to further enhance his already sound reputation on the greens.

The best the Americans could manage was a 4. Both made a par, in fact, which represented quite a save for Trevino, who chipped with a 5 iron off the road to within 12 inches of the hole. But it was a flash of brilliance that came too late. Cotton's putt finished stone dead and Europe had won 2 and 1, and once more the scores were level.

'I hope you won't leave us out tomorrow morning,' Cotton said to his captain, as he congratulated him.

'Don't worry, I won't,' Jacklin said. Trevino couldn't leave the scene fast enough. After a desultory handshake he was off and was back inside his hotel within five minutes of finishing the match. The only good thing, as far as he was concerned, about the match drawing to a conclusion at the 17th was that it was the nearest hole to his hotel bedroom.

Ballesteros, Olazabal v. Mangrum, Snead

In Hollywood, sequels are rarely as good as the originals. The freshness is lost and the characters who often seemed so endearing the first time around have become tired and stale. How different it was at St Andrews for the final match in the first series of afternoon fourballs! When the draw was announced no match was more eagerly relished than one that meant this repeat of the morning encounter.

Quite why Ballesteros and Olazabal were such a deadly pair was obvious to anyone who watched them for but a few holes. They complemented each other so cleverly and each relished so clearly the success of the other. The reason why Mangrum and Snead dovetailed so well was obvious too. Snead slammed the drives and Mangrum holed the putts. That is a crude simplification, of course, but a fundamental reason, nevertheless, behind all their successes at foursomes.

Now, though, they had tasted a rare defeat at that format. One could almost touch the determination to make amends.

What a match this turned out to be. Snead birdied the 1st.

Mangrum birdied the 2nd and 3rd. Snead birdied the 5th and 6th. Mangrum birdied the 8th. The Americans were out in 30 strokes, the best of the tournament so far. Yet their advantage was just 2, owing in part to some inspired scrambling by the Spaniards.

Ballesteros's golf had a fatigued look about it as he missed three greens during that outward half. But on two occasions he got vital pars to secure halves for his team, and a rare birdie at the 4th, accompanying three by Olazabal, at least kept the inspired Americans in view.

More birdies followed at the 10th, where Mangrum holed from 30 ft and Olazabal from a third of that distance. At the 11th Snead's birdie effort lipped out and he loudly cursed his ill fortune. Surprisingly, given the nature of the match, no player made a birdie at the short par 4 12th. At the 13th, Ballesteros closed the gap with a 3, but Snead's 4 at the long 14th meant the Americans were 2 up again.

Once more, this was now the only match left out on the course. It was impossible for at least half of the spectators still brave enough to keep trudging on to see anything. The number of journalists and, worse still, the number of hangers-on given armbands inside the ropes compounded the viewing problems.

But while the best way to see was undoubtedly to watch on television, there was something quite captivating about being there that made failure to see everything seem irrelevant. No one was prepared to march on ahead, whatever the difficulties.

The weary captains had now gathered around this match and several of the players as well. At the 15th a roar that must have been heard in the town itself greeted Olazabal's holing of a 15-ft birdie chance. Ballesteros once again wrapped an arm around his shoulder and congratulated him. Snead's look said it all: 'What in God's name do we have to do to beat this pair?'

The scoreline didn't alter at the 16th, where each player made 4. Back to the 17th, then, and the scene of Olazabal's brilliance some five hours earlier. The weather was closing in now. The grey cloud cover had refused to lift all day and so would rob the town of its last hour of sunlight. All four drove off into the gloaming, and all conveniently finished within 30 yards of one another.

It was obvious that Olazabal would try to repeat his morning heroics. It was equally obvious that he would fail. Such shots rarely fall twice on the same hole on the same day to the same player. Olazabal let out a laugh to himself as soon as he struck the shot. He knew it was bound for the Road Hole Bunker.

Ballesteros sliced his approach. It finished pin-high, to the right of the green. It was odds on that one of them would get a par, but who was going to get the necessary birdie?

Both Americans aimed for the fat of the green and found it. There was no conversation going on between the two visitors now. Ballesteros and Olazabal were still chattering away, however. It was Ballesteros who was furthest away but eventually it was agreed that Olazabal would play his bunker shot first. He came out to 10 ft.

How many times has Ballesteros chipped in or almost chipped in from just this situation and in just these circumstances? It is a tribute to his innate genius that it is no exaggeration to say the crowd expected a miracle. Ballesteros stalked the green. He assessed this slope and that, and then he was ready to play. A couple of practice swings. And then a couple more. He addressed the shot. He played it. It looked good, the right pace and the right line. The look on Ballesteros's face suggested it had a chance. It reached the flag at just the right speed to drop but there was no collision. It rolled 18 inches past and the distress on Ballesteros's face was matched by the groans from the crowd. Neither American, though, could hole and so the match was still alive, if one that the Europeans could now only halve.

The wind had abated now and so the drive off the 18th became a tactical one, with all players intent on leaving themselves the approach shot that offered them the best opportunity of getting a birdie. Even Slamming Sam could not make the green without the aid of a breeze.

From behind the green the scene looked magnificent as the four warriors made their exhausted way up the fairway. The last match of a wonderful first day had fittingly come to the last hole with both teams tied on the same number of points.

Olazabal it was who played first and he gave himself a birdie chance, finishing 18 ft away. Mangrum finished just outside him. Ballesteros seemed to take an eternity before playing his shot. Was this a spot of gamesmanship to keep Snead waiting? Whatever, when the shot came it was a beauty, and nestled 3 ft away. Snead looked at Ballesteros with something close to distress in his eyes. But his wedge shot still finished 9 ft from the hole.

It was as well that there was no possibility of extra holes because the gathering darkness would have taken care of that idea. From the stand to the right of the 18th fairway it was now barely possible to see the 18th flag. Fortunately the players were now on the green. There was no chance of a suspension of play.

Inevitably the Spaniards prowled the putting surface like a couple of gold prospectors. Ballesteros suggested that Olazabal's putt would break by no more than a hand's width and the junior partner appeared to agree. The putt did not, and missed on the high side. Mangrum missed as well.

With Ballesteros so close, Snead's putt effectively determined the destiny of this precious point. Hole it and America would finish the day a point ahead. Miss, and the match would be tied. Putting has never been Snead's forte. He missed. He cursed once more. He looked old as Ballesteros prepared to hole out. He couldn't bear to look. He had wanted so much to win and now he would have to settle for a half. He had no doubt that Ballesteros would get the putt. The enormous acclaim that rang out around St Andrews moments later told him that his expectation had proved correct.

———————

The captains congratulated each other on their teams' performance as they entered the media tent for the interviews. They sat next to each other on the dais. Jacklin was quite clearly exultant and spoke like a man high on adrenalin. While Jacklin aired his views Hagen had some Scotch from his hip flask. 'I'm so proud of my team. It was a terrific comeback. The Americans played some golf that was out of this world today and to hold them to a draw is quite something. It shows that we can live with them. The Spaniards were just tremendous. Cotton was just brilliant. I think we should salute both teams.'

Hagen looked a trifle disappointed. 'I said at the opening ceremony that I hoped golf would prevail and I think we saw that today. I'm a bit down that we haven't ended the day with a lead. I thought when Jack and Ben won again this afternoon that it would give us the edge. But you have to hand it to the Spaniards. Sam wanted so badly to beat them this afternoon but against those two it's like a rock and a hard place.'

The assembled gathering looked mentally exhausted as well. The joint interview lasted only twenty minutes. There were a few questions but most seemed to appreciate what a day it had been for the two men in front of them.

And then came the announcement of the following morning's foursomes:

Cotton, Langer v. Hogan, Nicklaus
Woosnam, O'Connor v. Nelson, Watson
Faldo, Oosterhuis v. Kite, Lema
Ballesteros, Olazabal v. Snead, Mangrum

6

Saturday: The Europeans Edge Ahead

THE RULES OF golf state that a player is allowed a maximum of fourteen clubs in his bag; a more accurate description might be thirteen clubs and a putter. The latter is the one club on which the players are all in agreement: they must have one. Even the driver is not indispensable. Peter Thomson once won an Open at Royal Birkdale using nothing more than a 3 wood.

Putting has come to be seen as a game within a game, which is hardly surprising given that roughly half the strokes a player makes are taken on the greens. A putter can atone for many other sins and not surprisingly putting has become an area of the sport that is often referred to as the black art.

Some players have garages full of putters; others have five or six chosen ones from which they select depending on the speed of the greens or simply on whether they are putting well or not. Some players never change for years on end. Some hardly switch at all during their entire careers and their putters take on a mythical status. Ben Crenshaw, one of the great putters, used just one through all his years of success, and it became known as Little Ben. Bobby Jones christened his putter Calamity Jane.

When a player is confident with his putting then invariably the rest of the game appears easy as well. Watson was imperious during his years of winning the Open. His putting stroke was firm. Look at an old video and watch the confident air with which he stood over a 15-ft putt. Often it would go 3 ft past but Watson wasn't bothered about that because he had absolute confidence in his ability to hole the return. Invariably, when a golfer reaches that frame of mind, he doesn't have too many back to hole. Watson had lost that confidence. He had started missing the short ones and once that happened the authoritative rap he used to deliver to those putts of 15 ft or more started to go too. Then the mental scar tissue accumulated and diminished the memory of the great years. But at St Andrews for the Ryder Cup Watson had felt more positive on the greens than for some time. He had been delighted with his holing out on the first day. He had slept soundly and with Nelson at his side was looking forward to what the rest of the tournament would bring. But those thoughts belonged to Friday. Now it was Saturday and the brow lines were furrowed and dominated his features as he took the police inspector through what had happened.

Watson wasn't quite sure how it could have occurred. He had practised his putting at the end of the previous day. He had placed his putter back in his bag. His caddie had carried the bag off to the secure hold where all the bags were stored. Now, as he prepared to practise his putting once more before going out, his putter was not there and it was looking increasingly as though it had been stolen.

To say the American was upset would be an understatement. He was trying hard to fathom how it had happened, and why it had happened now, of all weeks, just as he had found a putter once more in which he had complete faith. With just one hour to his tee time, what was he supposed to do now? What Hagen arranged was for all the spare putters they had brought with them to be shown to Watson for him to try. But only one was a Ping Anser and that a different model from the one missing, the one in which he had confidence. No doubt Ping would be happy to get him the same model but it would take all morning before it arrived at St Andrews. And would it feel the same? For Watson, like many players, a putter had mystical qualities, like a snooker cue, and if you found one you liked on a particular day you were damned lucky. Now he was being asked to turn to another, and he allowed himself a moment's depression.

Then Watson came up with a fundamental decision. He walked up the road to Auchterlonie's shop. He had decided he would buy a putter from there and use that instead.

Cotton, Langer v. Hogan, Nicklaus
The four players who would begin the second day's play were

broadly aware of what Watson was going through, but, of course, they hadn't been able to think about him for long. Indeed, if truth be told, they had hardly thought about him at all. This, on the face of it, might seem selfish at best and callous at worst, but really it was neither. Well, maybe a little of the former, but excusable for all that.

For golf is a selfish game. It requires long hours of practice to come to terms with its demands and enormous powers of concentration to conquer them. The four players who were now on the 1st tee had learned years ago that by now they had to be mentally attuned to the task in hand. They went through the rigmarole of handshaking and polite small talk with the starter and whoever else might be hanging around the 1st tee, but really they were thinking of what lay ahead.

The crowd were thinking about that too. Once more they had been on dawn patrol and once more they lined the fairway for as far as the eye could see.

They were wrapped up in extra layers on this second day. Several players had expressed the hope for the wind to blow to pose additional questions. Now, almost on cue, it had arrived and it was blowing at just the right speed: not so strong as to make the game a lottery, but strong enough to call for greater powers of imagination and ingenuity than had been required on the first day. It was a fairly cold wind too. Both Americans wore waterproof jackets over several layers of cashmere.

As on the first day, Hogan began the proceedings. His drive was right into the wind and travelled fully 35 yards less than 24 hours earlier despite being struck with similar authority. Cotton teed off for the Europeans. His was a good shot as well and the two balls finished side by side in the middle of the fairway. There was nothing to choose between them, and so it continued for much of the first few holes. Hogan and Nicklaus went behind for the first time in any of their matches at the 2nd, where Langer holed from 6 ft.

As Langer stood over his putts and adapted his curious method in which the left hand acts more like a crutch than an equal partner in the stroke, Cotton had two opposing reactions to Langer's technique. Should he watch through his fingers, so horrified was he at the contortions his partner was going through? Or should he gaze admiringly at a man who had gone through hell on the greens and discovered something to cope with the heat? Cotton, of course, finally decided that the latter viewpoint was the more positive and more appropriate.

The crowd enjoyed the early European success. The cheers filtered back down to the tee and beyond. People knew simply by the size of the roar what had happened. Then, as in a bush telegraph, they had consulted the person next to them, who passed it down the line. The four players had not reached the 3rd tee before everyone in the entire town knew what was going on.

The Americans didn't allow the momentum to build, however. At the 4th, Cotton and Langer were unable to reach the green in 2 and dropped a shot. There followed a succession of pars. Each shot produced feverish consultation among the Europeans. Cotton was the dominant partner. The watching Hagen could see the pleasure he was getting in trying to defeat two such high-profile Americans. When they had first met he had thought Cotton's golf had lacked polish, but there was a great deal to admire now. The two were firm friends as well, having discovered much in common.

The par 4 9th was downwind and Hogan's 3 wood travelled 370 yards to finish on the back of the green. Cotton hit the putting surface with the same club as well and, two putts each later, both teams had reached the turn in 36 shots.

As if to emphasize the wind's strength, the Americans hit 2 iron, 7 iron to the 342-yard 10th, which ran parallel to the previous hole though back in the opposite direction. Hogan holed the resultant putt as well. Two birdies in a row, then, and now they were 1 hole ahead.

The match would continue to the end with never more than a hole separating the sides. Cotton and Langer were proving an inspired pairing. The wind was largely helping over the back nine and they got the 3 on offer at the 12th to square the match once more. Surprisingly, neither side birdied the long 14th even though it was within range with two good blows.

At the 15th a precision iron shot from Langer finished 10 ft from the hole. Cotton sank the putt, the ball agonizingly circling half the hole before falling. Cotton's look to the crowd signalled to everyone what he had just gone through.

The 16th was halved in par and now the Europeans, one up, were in sight of a famous victory and the opportunity to go ahead for the first time overall. The two captains, sensing that the significance of this match went beyond the awarding of a point to either side, were prowling the 17th tee as the players came to join them. A grim smile from Cotton to Jacklin; no expression at all from Hogan to his near namesake.

Cotton's drive caused him to look in anguish almost from the moment he struck it. He had driven so beautifully all day as well. In fact it wasn't that bad, but it trailed a little to the left and he knew that Langer would be playing his second shot from the rough. In normal circumstances Cotton would have thought it satisfactory. But he had so wanted one more drive that was long and straight and true to put pressure on the Americans. As it turned out, it was Hogan who delivered what Cotton had been after. Langer was unlucky. Where his ball finished would normally be where the lines of spectators would trample the rough into submission. Not at St Andrews, though, and as soon as he saw the lie he knew he could not reach the green in 2, even with a helpful wind.

The object now was to leave Cotton with the sort of pitch that would give him a chance of getting the ball close for 3. The pin, as ever, was cut over the Road Hole Bunker, but not in the most difficult place. There was still a chance of a 4, Langer thought, as his ball came to rest 80 yards from the flag.

Nicklaus had only a 7 iron for his approach. He thought it unlikely that the Europeans would make a 4 from their position but equally he wanted to leave Hogan with a chance of making a birdie. It was a well thought out strategy and the shot completed to perfection. Nicklaus's ball pitched on the green and came to a shuddering halt 18 ft from the flag.

Cotton thought Hogan had a difficult putt to make considering the green's subtle slopes. He had asked Langer to leave him a full shot to the green because, with the wind helping, he thought it the only way he could get the ball to spin and finish close to the hole. Langer and Cotton consulted on where the ball should land and what would happen to it once it did: how far it would roll; what the resultant putt would be like. They were two perfectionists attempting to leave nothing to chance. Cotton's pitch finished 8 ft away.

Now Hogan felt that he had to hole the putt. Sure, there was a chance of Langer missing. But not much chance. He was very good in that sort of situation.

Hagen wasn't smiling now. He didn't want to lose this match and risk the balance of power transferring to the Europeans. Hogan wasn't thinking about anything but the putt and the fact he had to hole it or bust. His face betrayed no expression. Only his eyes moved as they considered the small slope to the left and how much that would affect the ball and how much to allow for it to still go in. Hogan didn't allow enough. The ball was off line 6 ft from the hole and missed by a couple of inches on the left.

Now Langer. The cries of 'C'mon Bernie' began from the moment it became clear that Hogan had missed. The 'Quiet Please' boards were raised. Langer went through his most deliberate of routines and, given the pressure of the situation, it seemed more deliberate than ever. People unwittingly clasped their hands together in prayer. Langer crouched over the putt. It was a good one. It was in the middle of the hole. But at the last it veered fatally to the right and caught the outside of the hole and spun out. Langer couldn't believe it. Neither could Cotton. Jacklin didn't want to believe it. The last hole passed without incident. It was halved, the match was halved, and overall the Ryder Cup remained even as well.

Faldo, Oosterhuis v. Kite, Lema

It was thought to be an unprecedented situation. Certainly no one could remember the last time it had happened. The American captain had asked if the middle two pairings could be switched so that the Watson–Nelson match against Woosnam and O'Connor would now be the third game to go out. Hagen naturally wanted to give Watson as long as possible to find a new putter. He thought it unfair to ask Jacklin if they could go out last because clearly Ballesteros and Olazabal were the anchor pairing with good reason. He thought, rightly, that Jacklin would turn him down. But he felt Jacklin would have no objection to a request for Faldo and Oosterhuis to play their match against Kite and Lema as the second game and again his instincts were correct. Once informed of Watson's difficulty Jacklin readily agreed and so a small piece of history had been created.

The players directly involved had no objections. No golfer so fine-tunes his thoughts that ten minutes either way is going to make much difference. In any case they were all sympathetic to Watson's plight.

Golf is famous for its sportsmanship. True, many corny claims are made for it and sometimes the language used is lachrymose to say the least. But the fact is, the practice grounds of any tournament are full of players helping one another, analysing each other's swings to look for faults that are sometimes overlooked by someone seeing the same swing day in, day out. Players rarely regard each other as the foe who needs to be defeated: the course is the obstacle that needs to be overcome. In match play, of course, things are slightly different, but no player on either side, not Brown or Snead or anyone, wanted to win so badly that they would have been glad for an opponent's putter to have gone missing.

Doing his mental calculations as to how the morning matches would go, Jacklin had Faldo and Oosty clinching a point from their match. In his head he had Cotton and Langer getting a half and although they had come within an 8-ft putt of a famous victory, he was still secretly delighted with the outcome. Now, though, was the sort of match that Europe had to win, he felt, if they were to reclaim the Ryder Cup.

Faldo and Oosterhuis certainly didn't lack confidence. Both were good players in the wind. Both felt a fast start was necessary against the Americans.

They got it, when Faldo's second shot to the opening hole was wonderfully judged, the wind hauling it back to within 12 inches of the cup. They went 2 up at the daunting 4th hole, where the Americans failed to make par. Both sides bogeyed the 5th and then the visitors dropped their third shot in a row at the 6th. But the lead was back to 2 when Faldo hit a poor tee shot into the short 8th. Both teams parred the 9th.

Lema had never played the Old Course in such a strong wind. During his Open win it had blown lustily on one day but from a slightly different direction. He enjoyed the challenge it presented. He considered the course eccentric but delightful for all that. But he was struggling here today. Still, he wasn't to blame for the Americans falling 3 in arrears at the 10th, where Kite drove into a bunker.

A smattering of rain greeted the players as they stood on the exposed green at the 11th and here Faldo knocked in a 25-ft putt for a marvellous birdie 2. He kissed the ball as he took it out of the hole and held it up to the crowd in acknowledgement.

The 11th was a good spot at which to record something special since all the matches had congregated around the Loop and so were within earshot. Jacklin felt the whole contest was swinging Europe's way.

A sublime tee shot from Tom Kite which finished 10 ft from the flag at the par 4 12th allowed the Americans to get one back. Poor Lema, though, instantly gave it away again by driving into the Coffin Bunkers at the next.

Faldo, by contrast, was driving the ball superbly. The indecision expressed earlier in the week had now given way to a smooth action and the watching Leadbetter chatted amiably to reporters who were following this match: 'I'm just encouraging him to get a little more zip through the ball. I think you can see that the swing is just a touch more fluid. It's looking very good right now.'

It was looking very good for Europe when Faldo and Oosterhuis closed out the match with a par at the 15th for a 4 and 3 victory. Kite looked particularly unhappy, and what were meant as consoling words from his captain proved no consolation at all.

So Faldo and Oosterhuis were unbeaten through two matches. Once more the most unlikely of combinations was proving fruitful for Europe.

Woosnam, O'Connor v. Nelson, Watson

Watson walked through the St Andrews crowds and left behind him whispered gatherings: 'Wasn't that Watson?' 'That's Tom, isn't it?' People recognized him all right but perhaps there was something in the purposeful nature of his stride or perhaps they were caught unawares, wondering what on earth he was doing there at that time: whatever, no one bothered him. Watson opened the door of Auchterlonie's, and went straight to the stand that offered a selection of putters. He quickly gathered three possibilities and, after a short conversation with the store manager, was escorted into the back of the shop where he could try them out. He settled on a Ping Anser, the same model as his own, but of slightly different loft and length. The store's professional carried out a couple of running repairs. Watson tried it out on the practice putting green. His stroke was good and he liked the sound off the putter head. But how could he possibly get the right feel in the twenty-five minutes that remained to him? He couldn't help but curse his luck and wonder: 'Why me?'

Nelson came over and tried to cheer him up. He had been too lost in his own routine to this point to pay much attention. Nelson had slept poorly and didn't attempt breakfast. Instead he pored over the notes he had made in his little black book of the shots he had struck the day before. He looked for particular weaknesses and whether certain irons needed specific attention and practice. How was his own putting? His putting was OK. He couldn't rate it any higher than that. Then again, how many times during his career had he been able to go any further? In a way, he wished it had been himself that had suffered such a miserable fate as a stolen putter. It wouldn't have mattered as much to him as to his playing partner.

On the 1st tee, O'Connor and Woosnam both gave Watson their sympathies. Watson's brief moments of self-pity were now behind him. 'The way I putt these days it won't make a jot of difference,' he told them, before breaking out into a familiar smile. All the same he was glad he didn't have to putt on the first green, where Nelson's attempt at a birdie finished adjacent to the hole.

At the 2nd, Watson found himself with a long birdie attempt and he knocked it fully 5 ft past the hole. Would that have happened under normal circumstances? Inevitably, the thought crossed his mind. He was enormously grateful to his partner when there were no consequences. Both teams dropped shots at the 4th, which, in the wind's gathering strength, was now out of reach in 2 strokes for all the players. Watson felt an awful lot better at the 5th, where he holed from 7 ft for a par to put the Americans 1 ahead. The Celts squared the match at the 8th, where O'Connor's short-game wizardry was once more in evidence as he holed a 30-yard chip shot.

This was another match that was becoming too close to call. The Americans did go 2 holes ahead by winning the 9th and the 11th, but then they lost two in a row after Watson drove into a bush at the 12th and then missed from 8 ft for a par at the 13th.

At the 14th, both teams took advantage of the birdie on offer. Here, Watson had an outside chance of an eagle and was unlucky to see the ball catch the edge of the hole and spin out. At the 15th, it was O'Connor who had the best opportunity for a win but again good fortune proved elusive, the ball turning away from the cup at the death.

Three holes to go and all square. Hagen felt this favoured his players. Jacklin did so as well. It had to be tough for the Europeans, having played well twice on the opening day only to lose both matches, to find themselves in another close encounter. Obviously no player wants to be defeated in three games in a row and inevitably Jacklin fretted that his pairing might try too hard to ensure it wasn't the case.

At the 16th, Woosnam's drive skipped to within a whisker of falling into the Principal's Nose Bunker before missing on the left. O'Connor's splendid iron shot to the green resulted only in more anguished moments for Woosnam as his putt, dead on line, stopped 3 inches short. The Europeans had had two chances to win here because Nelson had a 5-ft putt for a par. Both chances came and went as Nelson holed.

O'Connor and Nelson both found the fairway with their drives at the 17th and now considerable interest lay in Watson's state of mind as he contemplated his approach. In truth, there was little to compare between the shot Watson had to the green in that most famous of St Andrews Opens and the one that confronted him here. For a start he was 35 yards nearer to the flag. All the same, it was impossible not to compare.

What a morning it was proving for Watson! First the distressing business with his putter. Now he was having to relive this scenario knowing that the fate of the match all but rested on how well he executed this shot. In truth it was a good angle for him to come in on and in normal circumstances one would have expected an iron shot to remember given that the ball's placing called for his favourite shot, struck with a touch of draw. But when has the Ryder Cup or the 17th hole at St Andrews been about normal circumstances?

Watson selected a 7 iron. No indecision this time. A couple of trademark waggles, and a smooth swing. The ball caught the top of the Road Hole Bunker. It was an audacious shot to say the least. Would it bounce on towards the flag or roll back into the sand? In the event it did neither, and remained perched on top of the bunker. It would have been impossible to believe that a ball could stop where it had but here was the proof. The top of the bank had killed the ball's momentum stone dead and it was now lying on the three inches or so of flat land that existed in that particular region of the green. Woosnam's reply was more conservative but a good shot nevertheless, finishing safely in the middle of the green. Both teams needed two putts to complete the hole.

The 18th didn't separate the sides either. O'Connor played a delightful chip-and-run shot through the Valley of Sin but Woosnam couldn't hole the resultant 12-ft putt. The Americans never looked likely to make anything but a par. During breakfast Hagen had thought this was a match his men would win but given how the morning had gone he was not unhappy with a half. It left each of the four players looking for their first win in the event but for the Americans there was at least the consolation of knowing that neither had they tasted defeat.

Ballesteros, Olazabal v. Snead, Mangrum

This was a match that was destined to take place for a third time. How could the two captains have avoided it? They knew it had become a contest of wills between two very proud partnerships. They knew there was an element of machismo involved as well. Both Hagen and Jacklin had toyed with putting their men out in a different order. Both had talked it over with the respective players. Both had been knocked down. After all, when there's a bit of machismo involved how can you argue with a Spaniard like Ballesteros or a redneck like Snead?

To be fair to both, each had made a valid point which had swayed the respective captains. Jacklin had said to Ballesteros that he didn't want the match to be about anything more than golf. Ballesteros had replied that for him the Ryder Cup had always been about more than golf. If he and Olazabal went out third in the order then it would give the Americans a morale boost straight away and make it very difficult for whichever pairing had the anchor role.

'You know Seve and Ollie are going to go out last. You don't want to play them again, do you?', Hagen had said to Snead and Mangrum. The latter didn't get the chance to answer.

'You're not suggesting that we run chicken from them, are you?', Snead asked. 'Of course I want to play them again. I want to play them again now more than ever.'

Snead was to get the opportunity to square the series. The weather was against him, he knew that. The wind was now gusting up towards a moderate gale and was cold with it. If there was one thing Snead hated it was playing in the cold.

At the 2nd, Ballesteros's approach shot never got above head height. On his follow-through the club never got beyond the parallel. It was the shot of a master, and one learned on the windy shores of his native northern Spain. His ball finished 6 ft from the flag and Olazabal holed, which meant that Europe had led early on in each match, a direct contrast to the opening day when they had been behind at such a stage.

The Americans had made a good par at the 4th, though, to square the match as Snead's determination to win overcame his dislike for the conditions. At the 6th the Americans went 1 up as the Spaniards dropped another shot. Both sides bogeyed the 7th. The 8th and the 9th were halved but Olazabal won the 10th with a 12-ft putt for a birdie. It was Ballesteros's honour on the 11th and he was unsure what club to use. The wind was causing him to grimace as he looked at the flag and his caddie's yardage book, and he tossed a little grass in the air to tell him what he surely already knew: it was blowing hard against. He chose a 3 iron in the end, which was three clubs more than he would have needed under tranquil conditions. As the ball plunged into Strath Bunker at the front of the green, it was clear it still wasn't enough. All square.

At the 13th the Americans registered their first birdie of the round to go 1 up and then their second at the 14th, where Snead was thrilled to hole from 20 ft. This 4, however, was matched by one from their opponents as Ballesteros followed him in from half that length.

At the 15th it was Olazabal who accepted the chance on offer following a marvellous approach shot from Ballesteros. Both Ballesteros and Snead knew what the other was thinking – that this match had become a contest of wills – and both were relishing the competition. Their golf was becoming truly inspired.

The 16th was halved in conventional 4s and so once more the 17th would play a pivotal role in the proceedings. Both Snead and Ballesteros decided to hit 3 wood shots off the tee. Both located the fairway, Snead's ball finishing some 15 yards further.

When they got to their ball Ballesteros and Olazabal appeared to be taking on board the problems of the United Nations as well as club selection, so long did they take. In the adjacent Old Course Hotel there was hardly a window that wasn't filled with people watching intently. In fact, the only ones that were not occupied were clearly those that belonged for the week to the players.

Olazabal eventually decided on a 7 iron and frowned from the moment he hit it. The ball pitched into the side of the Road Hole Bunker but instantly it was clear there was to be no reprieve as there had been for Watson. The ball plunged down towards its sandy fate. 'Just find the green, Lloyd,' Snead said. He did. Snead applauded, and so did his watching captain.

When Ballesteros reached the ball he was less concerned than he had been when he saw where the shot was going to end up. The ball had spun around the bank of the bunker and come to rest towards the back of it, which at least gave Ballesteros a little room with which to try to weave his magic. It was still an enormously difficult shot and even more so given the context. But there was a glimmer of hope. In the media tent, everyone was glued to the television sets. The European contingent had let out a groan when Olazabal's second shot had disappeared into the sport's most notorious hazard. But as they watched Ballesteros and his reaction to where the ball had finished they began to become aware of the possibilities. The crowd wondered too whether they were about to see another example of the Spaniard's innate genius. The thought crossed Snead's mind, and Mangrum's as well. Olazabal was just hoping that he would get the ball close so that he could make amends. But at the back of his mind he knew that anything could happen next.

Ballesteros disappeared into the bunker. He was now out of sight to the people behind the green. All they could see was an occasional flash of steel as he rehearsed the shot he was about to play. And then a glimpse of his handsome features as he jumped up to get a final look at where the pin was in relation to his ball.

He was ready. With his knees bent slightly more than normal and the blade of his sand wedge more open than usual Ballesteros completed a three-quarter back swing and then a smooth rhythm through the ball. He knew it was good as he saw it just clear the bunker's terrifying top lip. He knew it would be close as he pictured where it was going to land. He knew it was very good as he heard the fantastic roar of acclaim. And then he knew it had gone in. The crowd told him as much and as he rushed out of the bunker he saw in one eye the joyous sight of Olazabal with his arms in the air coming to embrace him and out of the other he saw Snead with his chin against his chest.

As he stamped his feet to clear his spikes of traces of sand

Olazabal caught him in his arms and as he looked up Ballesteros caught Snead's eye and he wondered whether Snead would have enough resolve left to hole the 35-ft putt he had to negotiate. But he saw something else as well: he saw Snead nodding in his direction, and acknowledging that he had been a witness to one of the greatest shots that the game had ever seen.

Snead missed the putt and the Americans could only halve the 18th to lose the match by 1 hole.

As things turned out, neither Snead nor Mangrum, nor Ballesteros or Olazabal, would play the anchor role in the afternoon fourballs. Both captains had decided on evasive action, thinking that the other would not. How funny it would have been if both Hagen and Jacklin had put them out third in the batting order. But only the Americans would occupy that slot. Ballesteros and Olazabal would go out second.

And so this great series of matches between four of the game's best-ever exponents had come to a suitably momentous conclusion. It was hard not to feel a touch sorry for the Americans, who didn't deserve to emerge from the three without a single win. But equally, at the death, there had been a recognition that occasionally one has to bow the knee, and when it is because of genius then there is no blame to attach, and no shame.

Inevitably, Ballesteros's bunker shot dominated the captains' short interviews at the half-way stage. Jacklin thought it among the top three shots he had ever seen: 'I thought yesterday's shot by José at that hole would take some beating in this Ryder Cup but what can you say about Seve? There's no one else who could have done that. No one.

'I'm proud of all the lads. The match was swinging our way anyway but that last game confirmed it. We've got our noses in front and somehow we've got to keep it that way. I've said all along that we could do with being a couple of points ahead going into the final day because that has always been the strongest part of the Americans' play. But my lads are buoyant right now. They will have all seen Seve's shot on television. It will have given them a hell of a lift.'

Hagen was disappointed. He said so, but really there was no need. Disappointment was etched clearly on his face. He thought the conditions had favoured the Europeans. 'This is one of those courses where the more you play the more you know and I really feel the experience of playing it in a tough wind showed this morning.

'Obviously we've made it tough on ourselves. We're 2 points behind and we need to make an impression this afternoon or we're going to leave ourselves with too much to do tomorrow. But I remain confident we can do it.'

The town of St Andrews hummed as people talked about that bunker shot and digested the morning's events. They debated and anticipated what would happen after lunch, with these four fourballs matches to chew over:

> Barnes, Gallacher v. Nelson, Nicklaus
> Ballesteros, Olazabal v. Palmer, Trevino
> Brown, Lyle v. Snead, Mangrum
> Faldo, Cotton v. Sarazen, Casper

There was certainly much to debate. For the Europeans, the revered Faldo–Oosterhuis combination had been split up despite their morning success; so too Cotton and Langer despite a memorable half against Hogan and Nicklaus. For the Americans there was even more swapping and changing to mull over: just one of the original pairings had survived.

Hagen had asked Hogan whether he wanted to play again in the afternoon but in the end had made up his mind for him. He wanted him fresh for the singles. Halfway through the morning, when he had to submit his selections, he felt it hadn't looked too bad for his team and he thought that if they went into the singles all square then they would definitely win. He also felt that two of his partnerships hadn't quite clicked. Did Trevino need an exuberant partner to get him going? If he did, then he clearly wasn't going to get much inspiration from Casper. Perhaps he would do better when teamed with Sarazen, who was equally single-minded. Hagen felt that Nelson was playing too well to be left out, but Watson had asked for the afternoon off to work on his putting stroke. He had been pleased with the way it had held up to the morning's trauma but felt that another match followed by one the following day would be stretching his ability to cope mentally.

Jacklin had thought about refusing Langer's request to be excused a second match in the strong wind. His pairing with Cotton had been inspirational. The positive thing from Jacklin's point of view, as far as he could see, was that even if he rested Woosnam and O'Connor, he still had ten players to choose from and only eight spots. He felt he had to give Barnes and Gallacher a second game, and Brown and Lyle couldn't be left out after their showing on the first day. Ballesteros and Olazabal were automatic selections. So given these options Jacklin took into account Langer's request because he felt he had to play the Open champion Faldo, who was at the peak of his form.

It wasn't his style to make unnecessary changes to his line-up, but, taking everything into consideration, he didn't feel any unease about how things had turned out. He thought about the four matches in prospect and thought the most likely result would be two apiece. And if that happened, he thought to himself, we really are a good step along the way to victory.

Barnes, Gallacher v. Nelson, Nicklaus

Number one is a lonely place to be, whatever the sport and whatever the circumstances. In the Ryder Cup fourballs it often means shouldering the responsibility of getting your team either back in the match or further out in front. On the second day this was no exception, with Europe looking to establish a substantial 3-point lead. With just 4 points at stake all afternoon, it was clear, therefore, that the Americans were looking to Nelson and Nicklaus to at the very least avoid that possibility or, more optimistically, halve the deficit.

There was certainly no sign over the opening holes that the deficit would be reduced, with the determination of the Scots to make amends for what had happened on the first day all too clear. A birdie from Gallacher at the 1st and the only par managed by either side at the 4th by Barnes gave them a 2-hole advantage. The morning's rest looked to have served the home pair well. There's nothing more wearing than playing in the wind and both Nicklaus and Nelson had been involved in hard matches. Neither player could manage a birdie in the first eight holes, and by the time Nicklaus knocked in an 8-ft putt for a 3 at the 9th they were 3 down. Barnes had birdied the 8th, and he followed that by cancelling out Nicklaus's birdie on the last hole of the outward half.

There were no smiles from Hagen now. Nor when Nelson couldn't capitalize on a magnificent 2 iron into the wind at the par 3 11th that had finished just 6 ft from the flag.

Barnes hadn't woken up until 8.30 a.m. The first thing he saw was Nicklaus on television playing the opening holes. He had agreed to meet Gallacher for breakfast at 9.30 a.m. and both had decided to restrict their long-game practice to an absolute minimum, to prevent their swings being buffeted by the conditions. Gallacher worked for a while on his bunker play. Barnes wanted to perfect his chip-and-run, for he felt he could be playing quite a few such shots.

Jacklin had told them that they would be playing number one and to expect to be taking on Nicklaus and Hogan once more. Barnes, instinctively, had thought he would be wrong.

Now, on the 12th hole, as he contemplated a chip-and-run shot, Barnes was grateful for the extra practice he had put in. The shot finished 2 ft away and the resultant birdie meant that Nicklaus's two putts for a 3 did not allow the Americans to close the gap.

Their two opponents, however, could be relied upon to make a strong finish despite their morning exertions. Nicklaus's Ryder Cup record may have been rather disappointing considering his stature as the best player the game had seen. But never had he been so wound up for a Ryder Cup as this. Nicklaus had played through some of the years when the match was no contest at all, when hardly anyone had bothered watching, and he was never at his best in such circumstances. Nicklaus was always the golfer for a prickly situation, with a full house in attendance; those situations when the nerve ends are taut and a player becomes either inhibited or inspired. There was never any question as to the category in which Nicklaus belonged. Three down with six to play against Barnes and Gallacher was certainly a tough enough proposition even for Nicklaus. Nevertheless, he wanted to put pressure on the Scots in front of their home crowd and see how their nerve ends would react.

Two mighty blows to the 14th gave him a 4 and the hole. The 15th was halved. At the 16th, Nelson rolled in a 20-ft birdie putt but Gallacher holed from just inside him for a gutsy half. Jacklin must have leapt 4 ft in the air and Nicklaus was impressed as well. There was nothing wrong with Gallacher's nerve. The Europeans were 2 up with two to play.

At the 17th Nicklaus's drive was so far down the hole that he needed only a 9 iron for his second shot. Of the others, only Nelson found the green with his approach. Gallacher's 4 iron shot was propelled by the wind, unluckily, over the back of the green and on to the road. Barnes was slightly unfortunate as well. His ball pitched on the front of the green, and the bank killed its momentum. Worse than that, it rolled back as well and Barnes would have to go over the corner of the bunker if he was to get near to the flag.

Nicklaus surveyed the situation: Nelson on the green, the other two off it. There was only one shot he could now play: a hard 9 iron that flew right over the top of the bunker, pitching just 10 ft over it before coming to an almost sudden halt next to the flag. Jacklin generously applauded from the middle of the fairway. Nicklaus saluted the cheers near the green by holding up his hand, the club still held steady in his palm. Neither Scot could complete a miracle chip shot. The match would go to the last.

Again Nicklaus prepared himself for the big hit. He felt he could hit the green with a drive that sailed on the breeze. He was right. On and on it bounded before coming to a halt in the middle of the putting surface. It was some blow, and put into some form of context by Nelson, whose well-struck alternative came to rest 30 yards short.

Gallacher was a further 30 yards back, which left the way clear for Barnes, who, with his Sunday best, could probably match Nicklaus's effort. In the event he caught it a touch out of the heel, although it rolled sufficiently upon landing to finish in the Valley of Sin at the front of the green.

As the players walked down the last fairway, to be cheered every step of the way, it became clear to the quartet that Nicklaus would have every chance of registering the eagle 2 that would surely prevent a surprise victory for the Scots. His ball was only 25 ft away from the hole.

Gallacher was first to play. His pitch finished 8 ft away and was greeted with enormous applause. Nelson's approach was equally good. Now the crowd held their breath to see if Barnes could at least chip stone dead and increase the pressure on Nicklaus. In the event, Barnes elected to putt. Up the swale at the front of the green it came, but how quickly it appeared to run out of steam! Barnes's putt finished 5 ft short.

It was close enough, however, for Nicklaus to feel that he needed to hole. Do moments of past glory come flooding back at such a time? Of Nicklaus's two Open victories celebrated on this final green? Of the time when he joyfully tossed his putter so hard into the air that it appeared to touch the sky before coming to land leaving an enormous imprint in the hallowed turf? No. Only for the people around the green, not the competitors on it. Nicklaus couldn't afford the luxury of giving this putt anything other than his undivided attention. The familiar crouch over the ball. The seemingly inordinate amount of time before his putting stroke 'came to life'. And then the ball was on its way. Nicklaus's putter rose with him. He thought he had it. Haven't so many people on that awfully deceptive green? But the ball moved at the last gasp and it was enough to take it past the edge of the hole. Nicklaus turned away in frustration.

A minute later and his disappointment was complete. Gallacher holed to thunderous applause. Europe were 3 points ahead.

Ballesteros, Olazabal v. Palmer, Trevino

This match marked the half-way mark of the contest in terms of points available. What a contrast in the fortunes of these four players who had contributed so much over the years to the wellbeing of the sport! On the one hand the Spaniards were the talk of the town. On the other neither Palmer nor Trevino had troubled the scorers. Given that they had played just one match each to their opponents' three, this was perhaps not surprising. All the same, if America were to get back into the match it was clear they would have to start making an impression.

Trevino had been poor company for much of the previous evening. He had accepted his captain's invitation to dine with the rest of the team in the Hagen Room but he was gone by 8.45 p.m. and was watching television with his wife by 9 p.m.

Palmer was keen to score his first point as well. He knew that after another defeat the knives would be out. What better way for both himself and Trevino to dissipate the gossip than by defeating Ballesteros and Olazabal?

What a task they had been given, mind. The Spaniards were flying. There might have been only forty-five minutes between Ballesteros's heroics on the 17th and his opening tee shot in the afternoon but there was no sign of fatigue on his face, nor in his opening drive. Furthermore, the combination was again thriving when Olazabal knocked in an outrageous putt of fully 40 ft to birdie the 1st.

Olazabal continued to prosper. At the 4th he chipped in for the only birdie to be scored on that hole all day. The crowd were in heaven. The Americans were in disarray. If this match slipped away as well then that would surely be it.

Hagen had an almost pleading look in his eyes as Trevino surveyed a 10-ft putt at the 6th to get one back. The ball hit the back of the hole and stayed out. Hagen looked to the heavens. 'Is anything going to go our way?', he seemed to be saying.

At the 7th, Palmer had a 7 iron for his second shot. He took a characteristically huge divot and one instinctively watched to see if he would lean either to the left or right, which would indicate which side of the flag the ball was heading. Palmer did neither. He watched the ball's flight intently, and he liked the way it bounced straight as well when it landed on the front of the green. The ball bounced once more before colliding with the flag stick and falling below ground. Palmer clenched his fist. So did Hagen. Trevino had a smile as broad as the Eden estuary. Was this the moment the tide would turn?

Trevino knocked in a 20-ft putt to birdie the 8th and then Palmer drove the green at the 9th and putted stone-dead for a birdie. So did Ballesteros. But the Americans had gone 2, 2, 3 from the 7th and now the match was all square.

Palmer was perky. Trevino looked interested. At the 12th he chipped stone dead for a birdie and now the Americans were ahead for the first time. As Ballesteros's tee shot at the 13th plunged into the Coffin Bunkers, all at once he looked tired. The lines on his forehead were suddenly pronounced as he looked around and the wind whipped his hair away. Palmer and Trevino saw it as well, and they couldn't wait to reach their drives, both of which were in the middle of the fairway. Palmer hit another textbook iron shot. It pitched by the flag and ran 12 ft away, and he rolled that putt in as well. Now the Americans were 2 ahead.

Palmer and Trevino were 7 under par for the last eight holes and they were not yet finished. Another birdie at the 14th put them 3 up. It was extraordinary golf, the most sustained period of brilliance yet, and that was saying something on a remarkable day. What made it more noteworthy were the conditions in which it was achieved. Playing downwind was not much easier than playing into the wind because the players had trouble stopping their shots to the flag. It made no difference to Palmer and

Trevino: downwind, crosswind, into the wind. They still got birdies, and another one followed at the 16th, where Trevino holed from 20 ft. That, perhaps, was the cruellest of them all. Here, Ballesteros, forever the warrior, even at 3 down with 3 to play, had holed from 35 ft to sustain his team's effort.

When Trevino holed too Ballesteros looked downwards for a second but he was quickly at the side of the Americans to offer warm congratulations. 'You were too good today,' he said to Palmer, who replied with instinctive generosity. 'Well, Seve, it makes a change for the boot to be on the other foot.' The two Spaniards shook each other's hands as if to say: 'Sometimes you just can't win; it has been decreed that you lose.' It was a sad note for them on which to finish the team aspect of the Ryder Cup. By beating Snead and Mangrum in their epic series they had demonstrated their right to be considered the finest partnership in the history of the match. But no one can win all the time, and perhaps the unusual position for them of being considered underdogs had allowed the Americans to relax a little and return some of their finest golf.

Whatever, it had kept them in the contest overall. The first contribution of Palmer and Trevino to this Ryder Cup may have been some time in coming, but it promised to have lasting effect.

Ballesteros and Olazabal, by contrast, looked totally drained. The younger Spaniard had bags under his eyes, while the latter deferred any conversation with a couple of waiting journalists from his native land. The truth was that Ballesteros was absolutely exhausted and there had to be a question as to how much strength, both mental and physical, he could recover in the eighteen hours left to him before the singles.

Brown, Lyle v. Snead, Mangrum

If Snead was happy to have escaped another confrontation of wills with Ballesteros, he knew things were hardly going to get easier on that score with a match against Brown. At least he knew that on this occasion Mangrum would more than look forward to the encounter. If truth be told, Mangrum would quite happily have moved from the anchor role earlier if it had increased his chances of meeting Brown. Now he had got his wish.

Over lunch, it had been Mangrum, not Snead, who had been doing all the talking. 'Tired?', Snead had asked his partner.

'Not any more,' Mangrum replied. 'If there is one son of a bitch that I don't want us to lose to then it's Brown. Seve I can take when he plays like he did this morning. But Eric's not in his league. He's just plain rude.'

Actually, Snead didn't like him much either, and so it was that Brown's wind-up routine had once more got the Americans just where he wanted them.

As they indulged in the most abrupt of greetings on the 1st tee, Brown couldn't help but chuckle and recall the occasion some years ago when they'd gone through this routine and Mangrum had punctuated it by saying: 'Good luck, Eric.' It was the sort of thing that thousands of golfers have said to thousands of their opponents over the years even if, in fact, the last thing they hope will happen is for their opponents to have the luck. In the vast majority of cases it has been met by something along the lines of: 'Yes, you too.' Now Mangrum looked at Brown and awaited a similar response. What he got was Brown looking straight into his eyes and saying: 'Yes. Let's hope so.'

Mangrum had huffed and raged his way around the course that day and shook hands in obvious anger when he lost on the final hole. In the company of Snead, Mangrum had earlier swamped Brown 8 and 7 but that memory had long paled into insignificance alongside the painful one that came later. And then came the time when Brown had told him to move as he waited for the Scot to drive on the 18th tee. Suffice it to say that Mangrum's desire for revenge was far from spent.

Perhaps it was the sport having the last laugh, but anyway, while Mangrum looked at Brown and Brown looked at the Americans, Lyle concentrated on playing the golf that mattered over the opening holes. A beautiful 8 iron into the 2nd left him with a 10-ft birdie putt which he holed. Lyle birdied the 5th as well to put the Scots 2 up.

The 7th hole was proving kind to the Americans. First came Palmer's eagle. Now Mangrum's second shot almost managed a similar feat. As it was, the conceded birdie earned them their first hole of the match. They were square by the 9th after Snead had driven the green with a 1 iron.

The 12th hole was hilarious in a darkly comic sort of way. Brown holed a 20-ft putt for a birdie 3. Mangrum was furious. His second shot had finished 8 ft away and he thought he would have the resultant putt to go 1 up. Now he had to hole to prevent his loathed opponent enjoying such an advantage. Mangrum stalked the putt as if his life depended on it. He flung his cigarette on to the green and stepped up and holed it.

Perhaps inevitably, it was Mangrum and Brown upon whom everyone's attention was focused. Earlier it had been Snead and Ballesteros. Now, while the profile of the two players might have been lower, the confrontation was no less fierce. This was about as close as golf ever got to boxing.

At the 14th it was Lyle and Mangrum who both made birdies. At the 15th, all four players made bogey, an extraordinary occurrence given that the hole was downwind. Snead looked tired as his 6-ft putt never touched the hole. The darkness was closing in a little now. The wind was taking its toll. He was cold and worn.

At the 16th, Mangrum and Lyle made 4s. At the 17th, Mangrum sliced his drive out of bounds. He swore under his breath and lit another cigarette. Brown thought it inopportune to say anything. His drive followed broadly the path of Snead's and Lyle's down the middle of the fairway.

The odds were looking good for Europe now. Two to one, with the Scots possessing the advantage of having not played in the morning. Brown played first but he cut his iron shot to the right of the green, leaving himself a long pitch down towards the flag. Still, there was no hazard to negotiate. He told Lyle to go for it. First it was Snead, with an 8 iron. He expected the ball to roll much more than it did. It must have pitched 20 yards short of the green before coming to rest on the apron. Once more, he was in no danger, with no hazards to worry him.

Lyle chose a 9 iron and swung hard and fast. He had perhaps 15 ft to work in. The ball was heading straight for the flag. He knew he had to dice with the Road Hole Bunker but the object was for the ball to pitch on its downslope before feeding towards the pin. He misjudged it by 18 inches. The ball pitched on the very top of the bunker before rolling back into its murky depths. Lyle turned away and dropped his club. 'Bad luck, Sandy,' Brown said. 'It was a good shot, but don't worry. You'll still make 4.'

There was little chance of that as Lyle surveyed his sand shot from underneath the bunker's lip. He had a word with Brown and told him he thought he would have to come out sideways. Now the pressure was all on Brown. His pitch looked a good one but it checked unexpectedly on its second bounce and came up 10 ft short. Snead chipped up stone dead.

Lyle would clearly have to go for Plan B. There was little point going sideways now and accepting a bogey. Talk about death or glory. It was the former. Lyle was still not out of the bunker in 4 and disconsolately picked up his ball and hurled it petulantly at his bag.

Brown couldn't make the putt and he couldn't match Snead's wonderful birdie down the last either. It had been a momentous effort from Snead, as memorable in its own way as anything that had gone before. 'Stay oily,' he had told himself, and that marvellous swing had indeed remained fluid. While his partner had got caught up in the lust for revenge he had sought merely to satisfy his own desperate need for a first win in the competition. Brown even complimented him on his performance at the end.

'He's not that bad, you know,' Snead said to Mangrum as they prepared themselves to be engulfed by the media hordes.

Inevitably most of the questions were fired at Mangrum, but victory had enabled him to recover his composure and utter sanctimonious words. 'No, there's no problem between me and Eric,' he said. 'We both just want to win badly, that's all.'

Brown was upset with himself. He had played poorly. He had allowed his concentration to waver a little on the 17th. Brown had looked at the odds as he walked down the penultimate fairway and he had been dictated to by them, forgetting that golf, and particularly that hole, regularly came up with events that defy all predictions and probabilities. It was a moment's lapse that would stay with him all evening.

Faldo, Cotton v. Sarazen, Casper

Cotton was surprised when Jacklin explained to him that he had concurred with Langer's request to be left out of the afternoon play. The pair had formed a fine partnership and not only were they unbeaten in two matches but had played well with it. He understood more when Jacklin explained his dilemma. And Cotton had no problem teaming up with Faldo. He was hardly a personal friend but was someone whom he respected tremendously. Faldo possessed a work ethic and a desire to match his own, and while their personalities contrasted sharply, as did their public image, Cotton believed that his partner had many admirable qualities.

He expected them to team up and defeat Sarazen and Casper. Sarazen was someone not only for whom he had respect but who was also a friend. 'There goes Henry, a fine and dandy gentleman who has airs as well as graces and ideas well above his station,' Sarazen would say, mockingly. Nevertheless, Cotton thought that both Sarazen and Casper possessed a fatal flaw when it came to match play, and that was their unwavering belief in playing the course and never the man. This, of course, is one of those debates that has been going on almost as long as the game itself. Well, what do you do? Do you take no notice of your opponent's play and simply concentrate on your own game? Or is your every stroke determined on where and how your opponent stands or lies?

Sarazen was firmly of the former view. Cotton subscribed to the more popular theory that the truth lay somewhere in between. What, after all, would be the point, if in trouble, of simply accepting the situation and settling for a bogey if one's opponent was clearly going to make a par at worst? Then again, if you concentrated entirely on what your opponent was doing you would drive yourself insane: it is impossible to cover every eventuality.

The opening hopes proved the value of choosing a little from each strategy. At the 1st, all four balls were in the middle of the fairway. Here, clearly, was a case of playing the course. If your opponent makes a 3, good for him. But don't force the issue, and end up in the Swilcan Burn in gambling for a birdie.

At the 2nd, Sarazen was first to play with his approach and his 7 iron finished 3 ft from the flag. Now there was little to recommend a conservative shot to the heart of the green. Sarazen's shot had to be recognized and a suitable response delivered. Both Faldo and Cotton played aggressive shots: too aggressive as it turned out. They both finished on the back of the green.

So the Americans were 1 ahead, and that lead became 2 at the 4th and then 3 at the 6th with another Sarazen birdie. A succession of halved holes followed before the Europeans finally registered something in the gains column, when Faldo birdied the 12th.

Cotton birdied the 13th, so that the pattern of the match had been similar to a number played on the day, with one side establishing an early lead only to be pegged back on the inward nine. The difference in this case was that it was the first occasion that day where it had been the Americans with an early lead and the Europeans doing the pegging.

The home pair squared the match with their third birdie in a row at the 14th. Here Cotton struck two magnificent blows to finish just 10 ft from the flag and with a clear opportunity for an eagle. He was very noticeably distraught when he missed the putt but it was not to matter when Casper uncharacteristically missed his short birdie putt.

At the 16th Casper holed from 15 ft for a birdie but Cotton this time holed from 10 ft. The 17th was halved in pars as well, and so, as on the first day, the final match would again be decided on the final hole.

Again the players were fast running out of light. The wind had now all but abated and a haar was gathering. The conditions recalled one day at the Dunhill Cup when Faldo had asked for his match against Ireland's Des Smyth to be suspended with both players on the 18th. There was little point in his asking for such a thing now even if he had wanted it. In the event, Faldo played the best approach shot, finishing 5 ft from the flag. The Americans were 25 ft and 15 ft away, respectively, with Sarazen having the better chance.

It looked good for the Europeans. The last green may look flat but relatively few putts have been holed across its broad expanse over the years. Casper, though, added to them, enhancing his already considerable reputation on the greens with a marvellous effort.

So again, we had a classic match play situation. One minute Faldo must have been thinking that he had his putt to give his side a 2-point lead going into the final day. Now he needed to hole to prevent the day ending how it had begun: with the teams deadlocked.

Jacklin thought to himself: 'This is the man who I would like to have in this situation if I had a choice.' It proved a correct appraisal. Faldo holed.

———————————

It was a little while before the captains made their way into the media tent. For a start, there was the singles order to be sorted out.

Both Hagen and Jacklin wanted to consult with their teams. Both men had similar plans. Pack the top of the batting order with in-form players. Try to hide those who were not playing so well in the middle before finishing strongly, keeping at least one top man back at the end in case it went down to the wire.

Jacklin asked for volunteers to go out first. Woosnam volunteered, as the captain had hoped. Who would go out last? That was a tough one for Jacklin. He thought about Ballesteros, his young comrade in arms Olazabal, and he thought about Brown and Cotton and Langer. But eventually he asked Faldo to do the job and was delighted when he accepted. In the Hagen Room exactly the same conversation was taking place, although the captain knew instinctively with whom he would like to top and tail his team. It was just a case of sorting out which way round they played.

Into the press room the two captains marched. They were asked to comment on the day's play and Jacklin spoke first. 'Obviously we are very pleased. We knew it was going to be very tough but if someone had offered us a 1-point lead at the start of the day, we'd have taken it. When I looked out of the window this morning I smiled a little to myself because I thought these conditions would be more to our liking. But it's been a tiring day, an exhausting day, and one where we've seen any number of absolutely brilliant shots. There was Seve's miracle bunker shot this morning and that wonderful finish from Sam this afternoon when it looked as if the point was ours. I think it reflects great credit on all the players. I think every match or something like it has been decided in several shots under par and that just shows how good these guys are.'

Hagen said: 'All the players were a bit down at lunch time. We didn't come here to be 2 points down at that stage in the match and so obviously the objective was to haul ourselves back into it this afternoon. I think my players responded. I think you saw what character they possess, and it has set it up just fine for tomorrow. You couldn't ask for a better prospect.

'I can't think that there will be more than a couple of points in it. I think a fast start is essential but clearly we both think that, looking down the draw for tomorrow. Ladies and gentlemen, it's going to be a great day.'

And so, with the captains looking as if they were on their last legs, it was left to the press officer to read out the draw for twelve eagerly anticipated singles matches:

> Woosnam v. Nicklaus
> Ballesteros v. Palmer
> Olazabal v. Snead
> Brown v. Trevino
> O'Connor v. Watson
> Gallacher v. Kite
> Lyle v. Lema
> Oosterhuis v. Mangrum
> Barnes v. Casper
> Cotton v. Sarazen
> Langer v. Nelson
> Faldo v. Hogan

7

Sunday: The Final Day

Concorde's sleek and slender shape broke the morning's silence at St Andrews. It was 7.30 a.m. and its attendant roar was the perfect alarm call. The aeroplane was on its way to land at Leuchars, and in twelve hours or so it would depart with the American team on board.

As on the previous Sunday, it was as if the pilot could not resist a subtle diversion to have an aerial peek at the Old Course. What a sublime sight this must have been on this of all mornings, with hardly a cloud to disturb the uninterrupted vision of blue.

On the ground, the town was just beginning to come to its feet. No dawn patrol today. The first tee-off was not until 11 a.m. In the area in front of the 18th green a makeshift church service took place at 8 a.m. About a hundred souls attended and Bernhard Langer read the sermon. Casper was there, and Cotton as well. By 9 a.m. the first spectators were making their way through the gates to book their places in the grandstands.

More sightings of competitors who would shape the day's events were shortly to be made. Ballesteros was the first to arrive on the practice ground, and then Woosnam and Nicklaus, the protagonists in the opening singles match.

The air possessed an autumnal crispness but otherwise it was unseasonably balmy. Woosnam struck only half a dozen shots before removing his sweater and replacing it with a sleeveless one. The Europeans were dressed in red sweaters with white polo shirts and grey trousers. The Americans wore fawn pullovers with dark blue trousers.

It was 10.30 a.m. when Woosnam and Nicklaus were called

from the practice ground. They exchanged a few words and smiles as they went. As Woosnam prepared to leave, he heard Ballesteros calling to him. He turned round and walked back a few steps, and the Spaniard whispered something in his ear. Woosnam never did reveal what he said.

Woosnam v. Nicklaus

For the players there is much to anticipate in a Ryder Cup. Although the game now possesses a plethora of team competitions there is nothing like this one, the original, the one occasion when the players concerned forget individualism and think instead like a team. The camaraderie involved is considerable and the match can inspire amazing feats of bravery.

You think bravery too strong a word to use in a sporting context? Well, maybe. But courage surely takes different forms apart from simply being brave enough to stand up to a knife-wielding mugger or going to war. It is a form of courage to bat first for your team in the singles matches of the Ryder Cup.

And yet Woosnam was no longer a great fan of the event. He thought the hype overdone and the rewards too few for the effort put in. 'Think about it,' he confided one evening to a startled O'Connor. 'If you're playing in a stroke play event and you lose, then people write about the winner. But if you lose in this event you get hammered. What's the difference? I'm trying my hardest in the Ryder Cup and if I get beaten, well then, that shouldn't lead to all this abuse. Yet it does, and I'm not sure I like this event any more.'

Woosnam had a point. But as he prepared to take on Nicklaus those thoughts were forgotten. In any case, this was one match he could lose without fear of media retribution. Was that why he had asked to go out first?

Not really. Woosnam enjoyed the responsibility that came with trying to give his team a good start. He thought he would be playing Nicklaus and he liked the fact that the odds would be against him because he had been fighting similar odds most of his life. In his teenage years he had done a little boxing. Now he retained the mental approach he had taken into the ring: the bigger they come, the harder they fall.

Nicklaus, though, imposed himself on the game from the start. At the 2nd, his wedge approach left him with a 3-ft birdie putt.

The American got a 3 at the 3rd as well and a birdie at the long 5th. At the 7th he recorded his fourth birdie and when Woosnam dropped a shot at the 8th he was 5 up.

An ignominious defeat of record proportions was now confronting Woosnam. The crowd following the match had thinned considerably since the opening holes. They missed Woosnam's fightback.

He almost drove both the 9th and the 10th holes, needing straightforward chip shots at both after enormous tee shots. Nicklaus birdied the 10th as well but Woosnam got it back to 3 at the 11th, where his opponent dropped his first stroke of the round.

Woosnam entertained thoughts of one of the great comebacks when his pitch shot to the par 5 14th finished next to the flag.

It was as near as he was to get to the Golden Bear. Had Nicklaus mentally switched off, having played so well to go 5 ahead? Had it become too easy? Of course he denied it later, but he did acknowledge that he stopped going for his shots and thought more about protecting his lead than building on it. But he gave much of the praise to Woosnam, and the figures rather backed him up, for the Welshman was 3 under par for six holes from the 9th.

The 16th proved Woosnam's undoing. He had almost gone in the Principal's Nose Bunker once before. Now there was no escape. His drive flew unerringly into it, and he failed to reach the green with his second shot and registered a bogey. That was one shot too many against Nicklaus, and it gave the American a 3 and 2 victory. It was just the start Hagen was looking for. All square with eleven singles matches to complete.

Ballesteros v. Palmer

On a day that was sure to be full of cavalier deeds and memorable defiance two matches in particular stood out in the schedule. One was Hogan against Faldo. The other was Ballesteros against Palmer. One featured two players whose achievements commanded immense respect. This one, though, was a celebration of the game's infinite possibilities.

Already both Palmer and Ballesteros had demonstrated their sublime skills. Palmer had done so against the Spaniard. Ballesteros would clearly enjoy a chance to set the record straight.

Even on the practice ground they had attracted a great deal of attention. Even when they were just chatting rather than hitting balls people were staring at them and straining for a glimpse of that innate quality that both possessed in such measure: charisma.

When they shook hands on the 1st tee they did so with real feeling, and when an official photographer requested a snap the pair instinctively put an arm around each other's shoulder.

Palmer drove off first, that familiar flailing action. Even now, as middle age approached, Palmer remained a beautiful driver of the ball. Invariably his tee shots flew ruler straight. The blue sky framed his ball perfectly as it never veered either to left or right and came down some 280 yards from the tee.

Ballesteros chose to hit a 3 wood. This was done more for position than anything else. He wanted to leave himself a full wedge to the pin, which was cut in its Sunday worst position, just 10 ft from the Swilcan Burn. None of this worried Ballesteros. His ball pitched 2 ft from the flag and an enormous roar gathered in the throats of the spectators. Now Palmer, with a sand wedge. His ball pitched just behind the flag and came to rest 6 inches away.

Ballesteros acknowledged the splendour of the response. Not so much, though, that it caused him to miss his putt.

The pair shared birdies at the 5th as well, where Ballesteros was safely on the green in 2. Palmer chipped 10 ft past the hole but secured parity with an authoritative stroke. At the 6th, Ballesteros went ahead after Palmer drove into one of the unnamed bunkers that line the right-hand side of the fairway. At the 7th, Ballesteros went further in front where Palmer followed his eagle of the previous day with an ugly approach that was nearer the 11th pin than the one to which he was aiming. He 3-putted.

Palmer frowned. 'Can't afford to fall any further behind,' he said to himself. At the 10th, his 60-yard wedge shot finished adjacent to the flag to get him back to 1 down.

The two players shared a number of conversations as they made their way around the course. Palmer asked after Ballesteros's children. Ballesteros wanted to hear something about Palmer's business interests.

Palmer was indeed Mr Corporate America but there was also an appealing corner-shop feel to some of his work. Once, a couple of years ago, four journalists had turned up at the Latrobe course in Pennsylvania where his father had been the professional and where Palmer was now the president. Palmer had forgotten they were coming. Was he out on the course? Was he out on the practice ground? Was he doing a corporate day or fulfilling endorsement contracts? Was he doing a bit of hobnobbing or in a meeting? Palmer was actually in his workshop, putting the binding back on a member's driver. It was there that he felt happiest, and for all the adulation and all the fuss Palmer enjoyed nothing more than dabbling away in his beloved workshop.

The driver he was using on this day was a lovely old Toney Penna, made in the 1950s and worth a considerable sum of money. Its gorgeous persimmon head stood in marked contrast to the anonymous metal-headed woods used by his peers. At the 12th, Palmer's tee shot with his driver finished just short of the green. He decided to use his putter. Up the slope at the front of the green it went and down the other side. The ball moved not just up and down but left to right as well. When it had finished this rollercoaster journey it was clear that Palmer had judged it to perfection. It disappeared into the hole for an extraordinary eagle 2. The putt must have been all of 90 ft, and he looked positively embarrassed as he acknowledged the cheers. 'Sorry about that,' he said to his opponent.

At the 13th, Ballesteros restored his lead with a birdie 3, courtesy of an 8 iron second shot that finished 12 ft from the flag. Once more he couldn't hold on. At the long 14th Palmer's chipping was again exemplary. Two excellent wooden shots left him just 20 yards short of the green and from there he pitched the ball stone dead.

Ballesteros enjoyed a slice of good fortune at the 15th. He carved his drive right and the out of bounds beckoned until it hit a spectator and finished on the edge of the fairway. Ballesteros was not too concerned about that until he discovered whether the spectator was all right. She was. Luckily, the ball had caught her on the shoulder. Ballesteros got his 4, and a half.

The 16th was halved as well and so too the 17th, where Palmer's birdie putt from 40 ft burned the edge of the hole.

And so the patient spectators who had filled the enormous grandstand on either side of the fairway that serves both the first and last holes, having seen all the matches go out, were now to witness their first match coming home.

Palmer drove first. His drive flew as straight as his opening effort had done. Ballesteros's was a good one too, and so both were left with pitch shots from about 60 yards. The flag was only 8 ft beyond the Valley of Sin and it clearly called for a precise shot to get the ball close. Palmer chose the aerial route and finished 15 ft behind the flag.

Ballesteros selected a 9 iron with the intention of keeping the ball low. It pitched 15 yards short of the green. Would it get up the Valley? It looked to be struggling. With one final effort the ball hauled itself on to flat land. It ran several feet more until it was 2 ft from the flag. Another impeccable blow from Ballesteros. The noise was deafening.

As the players made their way on to the green everyone stood to salute them. This might have been a Ryder Cup and there might have been partisanship but Palmer was given a thunderous reception which he acknowledged with the warmest of smiles. And then came Ballesteros, with a dazzling grin fuelled perhaps by the knowledge that the worst he could now do in this match was gain a half.

Ballesteros's putt may have looked missable to some but not to Palmer, and he duly gave a generous concession. So the match rested on his 15-ft putt down the final green at St Andrews. 'Don't be short,' Palmer said aloud. As if he ever was. On this occasion the ball was struck a little too firmly. It caught the left-hand edge of the hole and spun out. Palmer shrugged and warmly shook Ballesteros's hand. And then the cheers began and Ballesteros saluted them all with his hands raised in the air. He sat down on the steps of the 18th green and awaited the outcome of the match involving his young prince, Olazabal.

Olazabal v. Snead

Snead had fallen asleep during dinner in the Hagen Room the previous evening. He had gone to bed at 10 p.m. and slept soundly until Concorde made its unscheduled detour and roused him from his slumber. 'Sheeit. What the hell is that?', he said. Snead couldn't remember the last time he had slept for nine and a half hours without waking up.

Clearly, he had needed the rest. He felt refreshed and ready for business. He had hardly touched his evening meal and so was famished going into the breakfast room.

Coincidentally, Olazabal was staying on the same floor and they came out of their rooms simultaneously. They exchanged restrained greetings. Olazabal was dressed in jeans and an old T-shirt. Snead was dressed ready to work. 'See you later,' Olazabal said.

'I'll look forward to it,' Snead replied.

Olazabal had been tired as well. The previous evening he had allowed his mind to wander and he thought of the break he planned to take in December and January, the long holiday he always gave himself at the end of each season. For a moment he wished it had been December there and then. He hardly touched a club for the first four weeks of his holiday.

Jacklin came over and had a word during breakfast. He asked him how he felt and whether he was ready for another 18 holes. 'This is the big one, Chema,' Jacklin said. They conversed for five minutes or so and the combination of Jacklin's words and the sight of Ballesteros ready to work had the right effect on Olazabal. By 11.20 a.m. he would be mentally prepared to take on Snead.

Jacklin felt this was one of those matches that would decide the fate of the Ryder Cup. Instinctively he had felt that Ballesteros would beat Palmer while anything from Woosnam would be a bonus. Olazabal's match was one from which he hoped to gain a half. He felt that if Ballesteros could defeat the mighty Palmer then a further loss for another star member of the opposition would have a demoralizing effect. Was Olazabal up to the task?

The opening holes were very even. The first three were halved in pars and while Olazabal bogeyed the 4th to fall 1 behind he instantly repaired the damage with a birdie at the 5th. After that he reverted to the previous pattern of accumulating pars. Snead never deviated from it. He reached the 10th in nine regulation figures. The match was all square. At the turn Snead at last got some reward for a succession of fine shots with his first birdie of the round. He birdied the 12th as well, but so did Olazabal, the Spaniard ensuring that he didn't fall 2 behind by following the American in from 10 ft.

At the 13th Snead dropped his first shot and now they were level again. At the 14th, Snead birdied. One up. At the 15th, Olazabal birdied. All square. The 16th was halved in regulation 4s.

Barely a word had been spoken between the pair as they made their weary way to the 17th tee. When they got there, Snead said: 'Well, I think we'll both sure be glad to be rid of one another for a few days, won't we?' Olazabal smiled.

Snead's drive flew exactly where he intended. Olazabal's response just drifted into the rough on the left-hand side of the fairway. Without the aid of the wind the 17th was now playing more or less its full length, which left Olazabal with a 4 iron to the green. He judged it well, the ball settling down in the middle of the green. Snead pushed his 6 iron a little but it got a favourable kick on bouncing and finished alongside Olazabal's. In fact the two balls were practically touching. It was impossible to tell which ball was closer to the hole and so the referee tossed a coin to see who would putt first. Olazabal lost. He putted first.

From 35 ft it was a long birdie effort and realistically he was hoping not to leave himself any curling short putt. At the back of his mind were the thoughts of the great deeds he had already seen here. His own second shot on the first day. Ballesteros's bunker shot on the second. Both in the presence of Snead as well. The putt pulled up 9 inches short and was conceded. No heroics this time.

Snead's putt was short as well: 2 ft short. He looked at Olazabal but the young man was looking elsewhere which told Snead that there was to be no concession. He was not too surprised. He would not have conceded it either. But he holed it none the less.

Could the sight of Ballesteros sitting on the steps behind the 18th green inspire Olazabal? Not on this occasion. The pair halved the last hole in 4s to finish all square. In truth they were both too tired to feel either disappointed or elated.

Brown v. Trevino

'Just get me a point,' Jacklin had said to Brown.

'You can bloody well count on it,' Brown said to Jacklin. He was in battle mode again, Brown against the Americans. It was the day of the Ryder Cup singles, his favourite day in all his professional career. And so he was to have Trevino as the opposition today, was he? 'Well, I hope he doesn't intend to chat his way round the course or laugh for the cameras because I'll bloody well soon put him right on that score.' If Brown had been from anywhere but Scotland and this had been the Open then the Scots would have been cheering for Trevino, no question about it. But it was Brown, stubborn, mule-headed Eric Brown, and they knew what made him tick and because he was Scottish they loved him for it. They cheered his name to the rafters when the starter called it out. Trevino cracked a joke and some of the crowd behind the tee laughed. Brown stared at them intently. 'Don't fall for his little game,' he appeared to be saying.

Brown turned his gaze to Trevino when they shook hands. He said nothing. What makes a player who has never proved himself at Open Championship level turn out to be such a winner in the Ryder Cup?

In one sense Brown wished he knew himself. Did he try too hard in the Open? Did he relish the responsibility that comes with playing not just for yourself but for others as well?

Whatever, Brown had never lost a singles match and he was determined not to start now, even if it had been something of a disappointing Ryder Cup for him to this point.

His start emphasized his combative nature and determination to do well. He made Trevino hole out from 15 inches at the 1st. Brown birdied the 2nd, 3rd and 5th holes to go 3 up. Again, Trevino was required to hole a short putt at the 6th, which he did, sarcastically, with one hand. Trevino wasn't cracking any jokes with the gallery. Trevino wasn't saying a word to his playing partner.

He did birdie the 9th and the 10th holes, however, to emerge from the Loop with just a single hole separating them.

Trevino enjoyed playing at St Andrews. He liked most links courses, in fact, where the ball was allowed to run and the shots to and around the greens called for that extra element of ingenuity. He demonstrated one himself at the 14th. He was 40 yards short of the green in 2 but played a wedge shot which never got more than 15 ft off the ground. This was because he kept his hands well forward and choked off his follow-through. The ball finished 3 ft from the hole. All square.

Brown fell 1 behind at the 15th after missing the green with a relatively simple approach shot. To say he was mad at himself would have been an understatement. From 3 up to 1 down was not the sort of golf upon which he had built his reputation.

He squared the match at the 16th, however, with a fine 20-ft putt for a 3. At the 17th his drive carried a little too much draw which put him in the rough on the left.

In theory this hole was made for Trevino. Start the ball out on the left of the fairway and let it draw back down the middle. From the off it was clear he had overcooked it. He had his hand out pointing right almost from the moment he hit it. Would it be out of bounds? A thousand thoughts raced through Trevino's mind. 'God Almighty,' he said. 'I can't remember the last time I was ever out of bounds.' He was not on this occasion either. His ball stopped short of the hotel's boundary wall with feet to spare.

'Lucky sod,' Brown said, under his breath.

Trevino's ball had finished in a horrible lie, however. The best he could do was to hack the ball 60 yards down the fairway, which would still leave him a 9 iron to the green. Brown couldn't reach the putting surface either from his lie. But he played a beautifully controlled shot to the right of the green, leaving himself a relatively simple pitch to the flag.

Trevino had to gamble. His 9 iron was a fine shot but it still left him with a 20-ft putt on one of St Andrews' most difficult greens. Could Brown apply the pressure? It was the sort of situation which he relished. His chip was a beauty. It pitched 20 ft short of the pin and then rolled out to the hole. His opponent left his putt short in the jaws of the hole. Trevino had run forward a couple of paces in anticipated glee and then he stopped as abruptly as his ball, dropped his putter and held his head in his hands. He turned away. Brown already had his driver in his hands and was preparing to drive down the final hole.

Brown's strategy was to play for a 4 and see if Trevino could come up with a 3. Trevino's drive finished close to the boundary fence on the right, which gave him a good angle to attack the flag. It was a splendid shot too, and it left him a 10-ft putt for a birdie. Brown finished twice that length away and he trundled the resultant putt down to the hole's side.

His 100 per cent Ryder Cup singles record now rested on Trevino's putt. Would he see the borrow at the end? Once more Trevino thought he had holed the putt. Once more fate denied him. He stood for a long time with his hands on his hips. Brown was saluting the gallery and being congratulated by the small rump of Europeans who had finished their matches. There were congratulations from some of the wives as well. And then Trevino walked over and shook Brown's hand.

O'Connor v. Watson

They set off from Belfast at 7 a.m. and were due home at midnight. Seventy quid all in to watch the final day of the Ryder Cup. Who could turn down a deal like that? Not the golf-loving, tournament-starved people of Northern Ireland.

The organizer thought he would be lucky to fill one coach. In the end he had filled five with no bother at all, and when they arrived at St Andrews their day was complete, for the prospect of following O'Connor and Watson was indeed enticing.

In Ireland the game of golf recognizes no border crossing. O'Connor was as popular in the North as the South. The Irish spectators were delighted he would be facing Watson, whose special affinity for the links courses of Ireland had marked him out as a kindred spirit.

They were distressed to hear that there was still no news of Watson's stolen putter. He had rung the St Andrews police station late the previous evening. The officers had gone out to the town's pubs to seek information but had drawn a blank. Ping had kindly dispatched a model that conformed to Watson's specifications but after a trial that morning he decided to trust in luck instead and go with the one he had bought in Auchterlonie's shop.

This was a match that drew its own enormous gallery as well, and not just because of the coachloads from the North and the sizeable Irish contingent from the Republic that was also present. O'Connor and Watson were two of the game's most popular players.

While silence reigned in the match ahead this one was played to the tune of smiles and cries of 'Good shot!' Indeed, there were many occasions when those words deserved an airing. During Watson's flying start, for example. After six holes he was 3 under par, 3 up, and had holed two putts of outrageous length. One was at the 6th and he kissed his new putter as he placed it back into the bag.

Many in the gallery were filled with trepidation. They wanted O'Connor to win, and if that didn't come about then they wouldn't be brokenhearted if he lost to Watson in a close game. But 6 and 5? Or 5 and 4? No, they didn't want that. No sir. Most of them wore sweaters from the clubs of which they were members, and the warmish weather allowed them to display their colours. Whoever has the concession to make Royal County Down and Royal Portrush sweaters must be wealthy indeed.

As the two players made their way to the 7th tee, a number of voices with Irish accents urged, nay pleaded: 'Go on, Christy!' Christy gave a wry smile.

The 7th was halved in 4s but at the 8th O'Connor won his first hole of the match with a birdie 2. At the 10th the cheers must have been heard in Dundee when he rattled in one from 30 ft to pull back to just 1 behind.

'Good shot, Christy,' Watson said, as O'Connor drove to within

10 yards of the 12th green. As on the previous day, Watson hooked his response into trouble and had to take a penalty drop. Everyone behind the ropes was now decidedly excited because O'Connor was back to all square. Or was he? Watson played a beautiful wedge shot to 18 inches, and so now O'Connor had to get down in 2. His chip finished 4 ft away, which wasn't a bad effort considering the slope he had to negotiate. The putt was a tricky one. For a second it looked as if it was going to miss. But it caught enough of the edge of the hole for gravity to pull it downwards. O'Connor looked mightily relieved.

At the 14th Watson went back in front with a birdie 4. The 15th was halved and then, at the 16th, O'Connor's second shot was misjudged and he finished off the back of the green. He got down in 2, however, and another hole was halved.

On the 17th, Watson elected to go with a driver and the ball nestled in the light rough to the left of the fairway, as so many had done before. O'Connor's was a beauty, straight down the middle. It was the Irishman to play first and it was a difficult decision to know what to do. One down with two to play: do I presume Watson is going to make 4 and so gamble? Or do I just play for the par 4 that every player is thankful to make on this hole and hope he gets a bogey? O'Connor tried to combine the two elements but his ball was drawing fatally in mid-flight towards the Road Hole Bunker. It finished up near the fence and now he had little chance of making a par.

This made Watson's task slightly easier. He now aimed some way right of where he had originally intended. He drew the ball a touch but that proved fortunate. The ball finished on the right-hand edge of the green. It was Watson to play first. With his new putter he judged it to perfection, the ball finishing 2 ft from the hole. O'Connor could only come out to 25 ft and missed. Watson replaced his ball but was not required to putt. O'Connor came over and shook his hand. Watson was now at peace with the hardest hole in golf.

O'Connor's disappointment was total. The record books would show that in yet another Ryder Cup he had failed to emerge with the number of points his talent demanded. Yet cold facts in a book can rarely tell the whole story. O'Connor had played well enough, better indeed than some players who had gleaned more points. Such was the cruelty inherent in match play golf. Whatever luck was present in this Ryder Cup it certainly didn't belong to the Irish.

Gallacher v. Kite

Kite and Gallacher were similar in many ways: similar size, similar build, similar outlook as far as the Ryder Cup was concerned. Equally there was a danger of overlooking them both as a little lightweight in this sort of company.

Yet both were inspired by the atmosphere and the feel of the event. Both were consummate team players who liked nothing better than being able to contribute. It was clear this was going to be one of the most hard-fought matches of all.

Over the first six holes they shared no fewer than four birdies. The opening hole set the tone. Gallacher's 9 iron approach finished 2 ft from the hole. Kite's response was to finish inside him. Two conceded birdies. Some lightweights.

At the 2nd hole, another precision short iron from Gallacher set up another birdie and the lead. Kite responded with a 20-ft birdie 3 at the 3rd to get back on level terms.

The American went 1 ahead at the long 5th where his superior wooden play set up a straightforward birdie. Kite went 2 ahead at the short 8th, where his 6 iron tee shot finished 10 ft from the hole. The 9th was halved in birdie 3s, which meant that Kite was out in just 31 strokes.

The 10th was halved in birdies as well, with the indomitable Gallacher refusing to be crushed. Here he watched Kite hole from 30 ft and indulge in his familiar clenched-fist salute. Gallacher was 15 ft away, needing to hole to prevent the deficit becoming 3, which, with Kite in such splendid form, would surely prove too great to overcome. The putt collided with the back of the hole and dropped in.

Kite was not to be denied. His seventh birdie in 12 holes came at the last of St Andrews' short par 4s and this time Gallacher could not equal it.

At the 14th he had a chance to cut Kite's lead, but he was not able to deliver from 20 ft. The 15th was halved in pars and so was the 16th. Kite was 7 under par for the sixteen holes played. Gallacher was 4 under himself in a game which hadn't witnessed a bogey by either player. In terms of scoring, it was the best golf seen all day.

Lyle v. Lema

It was interesting how the draw had thrown together so many players who were alike in so many ways: Faldo and Hogan; Ballesteros and Palmer; Gallacher and Kite; Cotton and Sarazen; and Lema and Lyle. Clearly, both captains had thought along similar lines.

This pair were the good guys, the duo who perhaps mixed most easily with the opposition. Lema, though, was an extrovert. Showing off in public came easily to him. Lema was never happier than being photographed with a champagne glass in his hand. 'I may look to you guys like I earn a lot of money but however high I get in the order of merit I'm always higher in terms of spending,' he said.

Lyle had earned the respect of the Americans in a number of ways. Chief among them was his decision to follow in Jacklin's shoes and pursue his career on the US tour. Lyle struggled for a couple of seasons. Many thought his placid nature at fault. Many considered he gave up too easily. But what Lyle didn't do was come home to Europe at the first sign of trouble, which rather negated the latter criticism. He stayed in America until he got it right. The Americans respected him for that. They liked his easy-going nature as well. During his early years on tour it certainly made for a direct contrast with Faldo, the other European who was most among them at that time.

Lema and Lyle got on well too. They had enjoyed dinner together on a number of occasions over the years. Lema struggled as well during his first few seasons on the US tour. One thing they didn't share was a similar background. Lyle came from an upbringing steeped in golf. His father was a professional and Lyle was swinging his first club at the age of 3. Lema's father, a labourer of Portuguese descent, had died when he was 3.

If the big guns at either end of the draw shared the spoils then the destiny of the Ryder Cup would clearly depend on which of the middle men could amass the most points. In this respect this match-up was crucial.

It was Lema's honour on the 1st. He shook Lyle's hand and wished him well and smiled warmly at the gallery as they acknowledged the starter's announcement of his name. Lema played the 1st hole impeccably. A sweet drive. An even sweeter second. The 6-ft putt for a birdie was always destined for the centre of the hole. One up.

As the Ryder Cup had progressed, so Lema had curtailed his evening activities. He had joked with Hagen the previous night: 'Do you know, I have gone to bed earlier each evening as the week has gone on. It is now 9.30p.m. and I'm absolutely shattered. One more drink and that'll be it.'

It was too. He was asleep almost before his head touched the pillow. Here was another American who was about to experience a nine-hour drift into another world.

Lema dropped a shot at the 4th, where his second shot finished in a bunker. He found sand again at the 6th, only this time off the tee. Again, the result was a bogey but he got back on level terms with a 2 at the 8th. Both players birdied the 9th to be out in 35.

Walking down the 10th fairway Lema recounted to Lyle his lack of social activity each evening but said that win or lose he was determined to have a late night that evening. 'Champagne, Tony, by any chance?' Lyle said.

'What a good idea, Sandy,' Lema replied. 'Are you buying?'

The 10th was halved, and the 11th, but at the 12th Lema registered a birdie 3 to go back to 1 in front. At the 14th, two wooden shots propelled by that wonderfully rhythmic action left him with a relatively simple chip and he put that 4 ft from the flag. He was now 2 up.

At the 15th Lyle responded. An enormous drive left him just a short iron to the green and it finished 6 ft away. One down. At the 16th, both players had good chances for birdies. First Lema from 15 ft. The ball never looked on line from the moment he hit it. He looked at the line again once the ball had missed and he smiled to himself as he wondered how on earth it had managed to finish where it did. Now Lyle from 12 ft. The ball stopped short, dead on line. Lyle turned his back on the ball and sank to his knees. An enormous groan filled St Andrews.

At the 17th, Lyle struck what could almost be called a duck hook off the tee. It careered into the heavy rough and from the moment he saw the path on which the ball was flying Lyle knew that he was doomed. He slammed the driver head into the St Andrews turf and said quietly and sadly to his caddie: 'That's it, curtains.'

Indeed, it was. Lema got the 4 necessary to secure victory. It was

the third American win in a row and now the gains built up by
Europe on the second day had long gone. With just five matches to
go the atmosphere and the mood had changed, and the momentum was with the Americans. A pensive look dominated Jacklin's
features as he watched Lyle and Lema shake hands. Five points to
be decided. And Europe had to win three and halve one if the Ryder
Cup were to return across the Atlantic.

Oosterhuis v. Mangrum

Trevino told Mangrum that if he couldn't beat Oosterhuis he
should kiss the asses of his team-mates. It was easy to underestimate Oosterhuis. On the tee he was hardly impressive. For a
start he stood 6 ft 5 in, which is way too tall for a golfer. It's like a
5 ft 6 in man wanting to play basketball.

Oosterhuis shuffled around on the tee, trying to get his posture
right, trying to get comfortable. He gripped and regripped the club
and then when he was finally ready he lurched at the ball rather
than swung at it.

For all that, Mangrum wasn't about to make Trevino's mistake.
He knew who looked the more impressive, the more stylish, the
more composed. He also fancied himself against anyone when the
pressure putts came. But when did style have anything to do with
winning a golf match? If that was all there was to it, how come the
big three in the 1960s were Player, Palmer and Nicklaus, with not
an impressive swing among them?

After his hyped up performance the previous day, Mangrum
inevitably felt a little deflated at breakfast. He still found it hard to
concentrate on the practice ground and on the 1st hole he duly
became just the second player in this Ryder Cup to suffer the
ignominious fate of finishing in the Swilcan Burn. A 3 from
Oosterhuis at the 2nd meant Mangrum was 2 down after two.

The American continued to make little impression over the
holes that followed. The next three were halved in pars. At the 6th
he had a chance from just 6 ft but the ball horseshoed out. At the
8th Mangrum rather made amends with a long putt for a birdie 2
but any satisfaction was muted as Oosterhuis followed him in
from 20 ft for a half. There was no change at the 9th either, both
players making 4s to give Oosterhuis an outward half of 34
against his opponent's indifferent 36.

So the halved holes continued. At the 10th and 11th with

conventional pars; at the 12th, where Oosterhuis made a brilliant recovery shot from a bunker positioned some 40 yards short of the flag; at the 13th, where Mangrum again missed a short putt for a win.

At the 14th both players had more chances for birdies. Ooosterhuis's effort from 25 ft was always a shade off line. Mangrum's frustration was reaching fever pitch when another putt spun three-quarters of the way around the hole but refused to fall.

Jacklin joined the match at the 15th and watched a poor approach shot from Oosterhuis finish in sand. Again the recovery was exquisite. The resultant putt was conceded: another half. He was still 2 up.

Oosterhuis was scrambling brilliantly. There was another example of his powers in this department at the 16th, after he drove into the Principal's Nose Bunker. His shot out left him with a 50-yard pitch to the green. It finished 18 inches away, and Mangrum was left to shake his head as his birdie putt from 15 ft failed to drop. It was the fourteenth hole in a row that had been halved. One more, and Oosterhuis would be the victor.

Mangrum had not had the honour since the opening hole. He could barely watch as Oosterhuis went through his unusual routine. But he was given hope from the moment he saw his opponent's ball passing over the 'e'; that is, the 'e' in 'Old Course Golf & Country Club', which is written on the landmark shed over which the players have to drive. That is right of the ideal line, and the ball was slicing sharply as well.

Jacklin's head slumped against the steering wheel of his buggy as 250 yards down the fairway a marshall waved a red flag to signify that the ball had gone out of bounds. Oosterhuis had a putt for a 5 with his second ball, albeit a long birdie putt of 30 ft. Given his scrambling over the previous holes, Mangrum half expected to see it disappear, which would have been some blow to him since he had played the hole conservatively after Oosterhuis's drive and had a long putt himself for a par. But Oosty missed and Mangrum 2-putted and so the American had won his first hole in the nick of time.

Both players hit good drives down the final hole. Oosterhuis's approach shot finished in the middle of the green. Mangrum's was the better of the two, finishing 12 ft from the hole. An unhealthy situation, to say the least, was starting to emerge from a European point of view. This was one match that had looked in the bag thirty minutes earlier. Now a seemingly certain win had become merely probable. Oosterhuis's long effort for a 3 finished by the hole's side. It was a good putt. He had left himself with little chance of winning the match wholly by his own efforts but at least he hadn't left himself a nasty short putt. It was now all up to Mangrum and his putt from 12 ft.

It was the sort of situation Mangrum relished. Experience and his own character had combined to bless him with a strong nerve when games were on the line. He even looked as though he was enjoying it all as he assessed the putt from all angles. Just as he addressed the ball he was disturbed by an incongruous cheer from behind the 17th green. He started all over again. Which way will the ball break? How hard to hit it? Silently he posed the questions. An eerie silence descended around the 18th hole. And then it was on its way. Mangrum knew it was in when it was some 6 ft from the hole. 'Take the break, baby, take the break,' he said to himself. It did, curling just as he had planned it, into the hole. Moments later he was submerged by joyous team-mates. Polite applause rippled around the scene. Oosterhuis struggled to find Mangrum among his peers to shake his hand. Mangrum, at once, remembered where he was and congratulated his opponent on his performance. The European had won the first two holes and the American the last two. It was beginning to look like that sort of Ryder Cup for the home side.

Barnes v. Casper

Barnes was a big man with a huge appetite and an enormous love of the good life, but none of these things was apparent on the morning of this match. At breakfast he sat there, eating little and struggling to make conversation with anyone.

'I'm nervous,' he told Jacklin. 'Brian, you're always nervous,' the captain said. It was true. No one loved the thrill of Ryder Cup competition more than Barnes and no one more dreaded the couple of hours to go before tee-off time. Catch him on the 4th, for example, and you'd hardly recognize the morose figure that now sat in the Jacklin Room and attempted to consume a couple of rounds of toast. Gallacher shouted good luck wishes and Barnes just didn't hear him. He was in a world of his own.

He had spoken to his father-in-law, Max Faulkner, the previous evening, ostensibly to talk about his win over Hogan and the man he would play today. Faulkner hadn't bothered to watch the play. Indeed, he hadn't watched any Ryder Cup since the rest of Europe had become involved. Barnes told him about his victory. 'I should bloody well think so,' Faulkner said. 'You've lost once to those damned Yanks on the first day. I didn't expect you to lose again.'

'How about congratulations on today's win, you old sod?', Barnes replied, jocularly.

'Just make sure you win against Casper. We haven't got a bloody chance if you don't.'

Barnes knew it was hardly going to be an easy task, yet he was glad to be playing Casper. In these days of players taking an eternity, he enjoyed his quick, unfussy rhythm; his habit of getting on with it.

Mind you, they had nothing in common off the course. Being a Mormon, Casper adhered strictly to Mormon laws and principles. Whereas drink never touched his lips, Barnes's rule was not to go more than a night without a drink.

He was incredibly serious about the Ryder Cup, however. He was desperately proud to have qualified for this team. And now on the eve of this match against Casper he spoke about his hopes and fears: 'Why am I nervous? You're playing not only for the team but millions of your supporters dotted throughout the world. If you make a mistake you feel you've let them down. That's it in a nutshell. If you get a bogey you disappoint only yourself really. But here, the responsibility is awesome at times.'

Barnes's nerves had largely passed away by the time he reached the 1st tee. A demonstrative handshake with his opponent, for whom the fawn sweater was particularly unflattering. In more ways than one, this was a heavyweight clash.

Casper's play over the opening holes could have come from his own textbook: 'Play safe and play within yourself,' he had told one journalist on the eve of the event, when asked for his credo. 'Golf is a game of thought and management, with a premium on placement, accuracy, judgement and finesse. I try not to be too impatient and greedy. I consider the variables, the margins for error, and then go for the percentage shots.' It was a sound strategy and wonderful advice to any amateur. But it perfectly explained why he was one of the least written about subjects in the contest. Who wanted to know about this sort of golf with

Ballesteros around, and Palmer, and Watson and Snead and Sarazen?

One of the things that particularly made it work for Casper, of course, was his imperious putting. He was at it again in this match. He hit every one of the first seven holes in regulation yet was never nearer than 15 ft at any hole. He had three putts of that length, one of 25 ft, one of 30 ft and two of 40 ft. Yet he still conjured up three birdies. Barnes had two of his own, reaching the par 5 5th in 2 and holing from 12 ft at the 6th. At the 8th he squared the match when Casper, unusually, missed the target and, even more rarely, failed to get down in 2.

At the 9th it looked as if Barnes would go in front but Casper's putting saved him once more, as he holed from 12 ft. With his early wrist break it didn't look pretty, but Barnes would be the first to vouch for its effectiveness.

At the 14th, Barnes's great length again told in his favour, when he reached the green with two mighty blows. It gave him a 1-hole lead. At the 16th, Casper clawed it back, with another single putt, his seventh of the round.

At the 17th, Casper hit a poor drive into the right rough. Barnes was off the fairway as well, but not as far. Now it was down to luck. Who would have the best lie? If all was fair then it would be Barnes, since his drive was nowhere near as astray. But when has golf been about fairness?

At least on this occasion it was. Barnes could reach the green from his lie. Casper hadn't a chance. In fact, he still had 130 yards to go for his third and was always going to make 5 after a poor 9 iron shot. Barnes hit one of the shots of the day. A 5 iron, drilled into the ether, that hopped and bounded on to the putting surface. The roar that had caused Mangrum to back away up ahead on the 18th was Barnes putting his ball adjacent to the hole for a win.

One up with one to play. Just like Oosterhuis. Europe could afford no further lapses. If Barnes had thought for a moment about his words before the contest, and how much they applied now, then it would have been doubtful whether he could have taken the club back. He was nervous, yes; but he was so concentrating on the job at hand that he didn't allow his mind to wander away and consider the consequences. Both players hit good drives. Casper's approach finished almost exactly where the watching Mangrum's had moments earlier. Barnes's finished 18 ft away.

Barnes felt he had to hole his putt, such was Casper's prowess on the greens. He smiled wryly to himself. What on earth was going through his mind to bring a smile at such a moment? Later, he said that he was thinking to himself: 'What I wouldn't give for a drink right now!'

If the watching Jacklin had known, he would probably have replied: 'You can drink the town dry if you just hole the damned putt.'

And that's exactly what Barnes did (hole the putt, that is). Two points out of two against Casper. He looked as if he couldn't believe it. Barnes dropped his putter and looked up to the sky and put one startled hand to his face. He dropped to his knees and kissed the green. Europe were still in with a chance. Just as importantly for Barnes: he hadn't let anyone down.

Cotton v. Sarazen

No doubt every person who was present to witness these great matches and all those watching at home on television both in Europe and America had done some mental arithmetic: they had calculated who they thought would win each of the games and so decided for themselves who was going to take the trophy.

But how could you call this match? The two players' records suggested a momentous struggle with neither player being able to intimidate the other. When asked what strategy he would use against Cotton, Sarazen said: 'The same as I use against every other player. I'll just concentrate on my own game and work on it to try to make it good enough to prevail on the day.'

It had always been this way with Sarazen. When he first started to earn rave notices he was asked about his philosophy towards the game. He replied: 'Your game counts for you and mine for me. In other words, look out for number one, because in doing that you'll find plenty to care for.'

With his charisma and his personality and the sheer quality of his golf, Cotton could often unnerve an opponent but he knew that would not be the case on this day.

At breakfast Cotton sat with his arms nursing his churned-up stomach. He managed some muesli and black coffee but that was it. He spoke little. The opening holes were predictably keenly fought with nothing to separate him from Sarazen. Neither man spoke more than a few words to the other. Their friendship was clearly going to be placed on hold for several hours.

At the 5th, though, Cotton chipped stone dead for a birdie to go in front. He displayed little emotion and his concentration was such that when asked later to recall details of his round he could remember little.

Sarazen pegged him back at the 6th with a birdie of his own. At the 8th, Cotton 3-putted from 40 ft but redeemed the error at the 10th to square the match.

At the 12th both players made birdie 3s with Cotton holing from 10 ft and Sarazen from half that length. Now all conversation was a thing of the past. At the 13th it was Sarazen's turn to go in front when Cotton drove into a bunker.

Neither player could make a birdie at the 14th but Cotton did get back on level terms at the 15th, where his iron approach finished 7 ft from the flag. At the 16th Cotton squandered a golden opportunity to go in front. The match appeared to be swinging his way as he followed up his success at the 15th with another splendid approach, this one finishing just 4 ft away. Furthermore, Sarazen had completely misjudged his shot, and had gone through the back. But the veteran American played a gorgeous chip shot that did everything but go in the hole. Now Cotton had to sink his putt. He lipped out and heaved an enormous sigh.

At the 17th, Sarazen was again in trouble with his second shot. This time he finished in the Road Hole Bunker. Again Cotton played a marvellous iron, his ball coming to rest 18 ft from the flag.

How ironic that the man who is largely credited with having invented the sand wedge should find himself in the world's most famous sand hazard, needing to play a wonderful recovery shot to have any chance to avoid being behind going down the final hole.

Sarazen didn't just invent the sand wedge. He practised with it and the updated models as they appeared so that he remained one of its best exponents. Was it a hard bunker shot? Given the bunker and the context it was perilously difficult. But as in Ballesteros's case the previous day there was a smidgeon of room with which to work and it turned out to be all Sarazen needed. It was a textbook effort, the ball landing gently and coming to rest 3 ft from the hole. Cotton missed his putt. Sarazen did not. Once more he had rescued an unlikely half.

Cotton couldn't nail his man at the last either. Sarazen had overcome unlikely odds playing the final few holes to secure a tied match, but then, wasn't that the story of his life?

Hagen congratulated both men. He had words of sympathy for his friend Cotton. 'A drink later, Henry?', Hagen said. Cotton didn't hear him, so overcome was he with disappointment. Hagen repeated the words. Cotton looked at the scoreboard. 'Looks like you'll be buying,' he said disconsolately.

Langer v. Nelson

It did indeed. Europe now needed to win one of the last two singles and halve the other. Nelson and Hogan were hardly the two opponents against whom one would expect to get such a result.

At least Langer was refreshed, having taken the previous afternoon off, and Faldo was playing supremely well.

The approach of Langer and Nelson leading up to their 12.40 tee-off time could hardly have been of greater contrast. After reading the sermon at the morning's church service Langer had enjoyed a healthy breakfast (that's healthy as in things that are good for you). He had talked and practised and generally behaved as though he were about to go out and play in the first round of the Joe Bloggs Classic. This didn't mean that he was taking it all any less seriously than anyone else. It was just Bernhard Langer. He knew how to compartmentalize the sport. He didn't allow it to rule him. When it was game on there was no more fierce competitor. When it was leisure time he knew how to relax.

Not so Nelson. He hadn't stopped thinking about his match since the previous evening. He had slept fitfully. Before practice he had once more gone through his black book. 'Anything I've forgotten? Anything that's going to particularly help me today? Eleventh man out? Gee, I can't afford to lose playing eleventh man, can I?'

He looked pale and drawn as he made his way to the first tee and his opening drive would have had him in trouble at anywhere but St Andrews. It finished fully 40 yards left of where he intended. By the time he reached his ball, however, he had composed himself, and soon the audience were to witness a riveting exhibition from one of the greatest shot makers, if not the greatest, that the game has ever seen.

Only his indifferent putting allowed Langer to keep a toehold in the game over the opening nine. Nelson's 8 iron to the 1st green finished 8 ft away. At the 2nd he was 6 ft from the pin. Indeed, over the first six holes he was never more than 12 ft from the flag. He made just two of those putts, a measly ration considering the peerless quality of the strokes that had got him into such a position.

Langer made a birdie at the 5th as well and so the margin between them was just 1 hole. At the 8th, Nelson went 2 up when he holed his longest putt of the day, from 18 ft. The 9th and 10th were halved. At the 11th, Nelson again birdied, to give his side a 3-hole advantage.

It was looking parlous for Europe. If they lost this rubber then the best they could hope for was a halved match, which would mean the cup going back to America.

Jacklin came scurrying back from matches up ahead to watch. He arrived just in time for Langer to give him renewed hope. He won the 12th with a birdie of his own.

Nelson was playing smooth, effortless golf with that familiar driving action through the ball. At the 13th he again knocked the ball close for 2 and again missed a short putt. At the 14th his pitch finished 4 inches from the flag. No chance of missing that one, he muttered to himself. Furthermore, it was a winning birdie.

Now it really was a desperate situation for the Europeans. Three down with four to play. One thing that could be taken as read was that Langer would not give up. Yet how could he get back into the match against a man playing this well? His only hope was to keep trying to place pressure on Nelson's putting. How ironic: the man who had come through the yips on no fewer than three occasions had come to believe that his only chance of winning was on the greens.

At the 15th, Langer hit a brave second shot to 10 ft. Nelson was safely home in par. As Langer stood over the putt, spectators in the gallery held their breath. They let out a great roar of relief when he holed it. At the 16th Langer came up 25 ft short of the flag with his second shot. Nelson was 15 ft away in 2.

Europe were looking for a miracle. Again Langer obliged, the ball practically doing a full circumference before descending below ground. But there was still Nelson to putt. The tension was palpable. The putt was a miserable one, finishing 9 inches short of the hole. Nelson knocked it away desultorily.

Langer's drive down the 17th was propelled by adrenalin. It

landed 310 yards from the tee, with little assistance from the elements. Nelson hit a good one too, some 15 yards behind. Both were in the middle of the fairway. Nelson took note of Langer's position but didn't feel his shot called for any heroics. He knew that if he made 4 there was every chance that at worst he would be going down the final hole 1 up, and that was a very satisfactory state of affairs. Also, he knew that if he could find the green then Langer would be under pressure to try for the heroic.

And that is what he did. His ball finished 20 ft from the flag, a wonderful stroke. He guessed correctly. Langer felt he now had to make a birdie. He had a 6 iron in his hands and instinctively he felt it a good shot as in flight he watched it dissect the flag. 'Get close,' Langer said. It pitched 5 ft behind the flag. But the ball didn't check until its second bounce and by then it was too late. It trickled down over the green and on to the gravel path before the road.

Langer was devastated. He looked at the ground for a long time. He looked at his caddie. He checked the yardage he had been given. In short, he couldn't believe what had happened, what cruel fate had just befallen him. He knew he had little chance now of making the birdie he desperately needed.

The chip was an inordinately difficult one. Should he run it up the bank, needing to judge it very finely if the ball was to get near the hole? Or should he pitch it on to the back edge and try to play it so deftly that again it didn't finish far away?

He chose the former. The bank took rather more out of the ball than he had anticipated. He barely made the green. Nelson putted up close to the hole and now Langer, who minutes earlier had been anticipating a birdie chance, had to sink his putt for a par merely to stay in the match. His mind was digesting all this and it was proving hard to concentrate on the task in hand. Langer backed away. He composed himself by having one more look at the putt from two angles. The putt had a borrow of two inches from left to right but it was easy to allow too much. It was a putt that you would normally see holed perhaps four times out of ten. Fortunately for Langer, this was one of the four. 'That', said Jacklin, 'was one of the bravest putts I have ever seen in my life.'

And so the spectators who had packed the grandstands that lined the first and last holes were to get another glimpse of the action. They saw two perfect drives, and two men who exchanged a few words as they walked up the final fairway. It was a lovely sporting scene. Langer walked almost to the green before playing his second shot. Should he play it through the Valley of Sin or should he pitch it all the way to the flag? He decided on the latter. The ball hit the flag and as a deafening roar engulfed the scene it came to rest no more than 3 inches from the hole.

There was no way that any words from Nelson would have been heard above the noise but he looked over at Langer and signalled his recognition of his opponent's achievement. How could Nelson follow that? Perhaps understandably, he played one of his poorest iron shots of the day. He missed his birdie putt. The crowd exploded once more with a cacophony of noise.

Langer waved his thanks. He had had four single putts over the last four holes and had won three of them. It was a typically courageous effort from the German to secure a half. And it meant that Europe lived in hope into the last match.

Faldo v. Hogan

And so it all came down to this. If Nicklaus and Ballesteros would probably get most people's votes as the finest players to have come out of America and Europe respectively, there would nevertheless be no shortage of supporters for Faldo and Hogan.

It was impossible not to admire the way each had selflessly dedicated their lives to making a name for themselves at their chosen profession. Such was their determination to succeed that their achievements had come largely at the expense of any popularity. But there was no shortage of people willing them on now, calling out their names with an urgency that reflected the situation.

Europe had to win this match. A half would mean a share of the spoils overall but that the trophy would return on Concorde to America. Faldo had instinctively felt beforehand that this would be the case and mentally he had prepared himself for just such a situation.

Hogan just wanted to win. He had volunteered to go out last. That morning he had gone through his usual routine, his compulsory morning exercises to get the blood coursing through his legs. Now in the hour that remained to him before he was due to tee off he sat alone and thought about the match ahead, and also his times in Scotland: how they had been few and far between but always special and frequently successful. He thought about his

Open win at Carnoustie on his first visit and how the people had saluted him. 'The wee ice mon.' He liked that. And as he stood on the first tee waiting to go he could feel their reverence.

He shook hands with Faldo and the pair smiled thinly at one another. There was so much they could recognize in the other's approach to the game. So much to admire and respect.

Faldo saw no need for any sweaters; Hogan just wore the thinnest V-neck pullover. A match that would surely be savoured on a day to remember. Ten minutes later, it had produced its first birdie. First blood to Hogan.

His wedge shot had finished 8 ft from the flag and his facial features never changed as the ball found the heart of the hole for a winning birdie 3. He touched his white cap in recognition of the applause. Hogan birdied the 3rd as well but this time Faldo followed him in from 8 ft. Faldo clenched his fist and many in the crowd did as well.

No words were spoken now, except between caddie and player as each competitor analysed his shots to the greens. They consulted about slopes and hollows and where the flag was and how far to the front of the green and how much further to the pin. Hogan had generally the quicker routine. Faldo looked the more relaxed as they walked between shots. At the 4th Faldo squared the match when Hogan missed a par putt of 6 ft. Again no emotion. Here there was a contrast with Faldo, when the tall, angular Englishmen missed one from a similar distance to win the 7th. His gestures suggested that the ball had cannoned off a spike mark and moved left. He tapped down the offending node but it was too late. He glowered as he made his way to the 8th tee. Once there, though, he had forgotten his misfortune. His tee shot again left him a short birdie putt and this time he holed it. Now he was 1 up. Both players accepted the birdie opportunity at the 9th. Faldo was out in 33, Hogan in 34. So far so good for Europe, but the opening nine had hardly provided a clue as to how the rest of the contest would go.

Hogan squared the match at the 11th where Faldo registered a rare bogey, after his tee shot had finished in Strath Bunker. Surprisingly, neither player managed a birdie at the 12th. Faldo had elected to take a 5 iron off the tee and then a full wedge to the green and never really gave himself a chance of making a 3. But Hogan was only 15 yards short with his drive and there was almost a flicker of disappointment in his eyes when he could only pitch the ball to 15 ft. Almost.

The 13th was halved in fours. At the 14th, Faldo miscued his drive and so had to play short of Hell Bunker for 2. Hogan was just short of the green. Faldo's blind third stroke finished 18 ft from the flag. Again, Hogan's chip was not one of his best, coming up 5 ft short.

Only in match play: could Faldo hole, so leaving Hogan, perhaps anticipating a putt for a winning 4, having to hole instead merely for a half?

Faldo did indeed hole. Hogan's putt never even touched the cup.

It looked like one of those defining incidents in a match. From a potentially losing situation Faldo had carved out a win. The crowd felt that things were going his way. And if things were going Faldo's way then the match in its entirety was going Europe's way.

But while the galleries debated the hole's significance and concluded that it would be looked upon as the moment when the Ryder Cup was won and lost, so Hogan hit another iron to 4 ft at the 15th and this time he did hole to square the match. He looked the same as he had walking off the previous green.

At the 16th, both players hit good drives down the left-hand side, thus safely avoiding the bunkers in the middle of the fairway. Faldo was to play first and with an 8 iron he pitched the ball to within 2 ft of the flag. The cheering had still to die down as Hogan settled over the ball, and for once the great man's concentration was disturbed and he had to back away. He soon settled once more over the ball. His approach finished 20 ft from the flag. There was no great cheer from the American supporters who were watching this match. Hogan walked implacably down the middle of the fairway. He looked neither left nor right, his eyes seemingly focused on the ball. Even as he got to the green his eyes didn't appear to be weighing up the possibilities, to be surveying the contours and the obstacles that stood between him and a birdie.

Hogan conceded Faldo's putt. He placed his own ball down and at last gave an outward sign that he was considering what lay ahead. He didn't take long to look over the putt. He was soon crouched over it. The ball had 6 ft to travel when he started walking after it. Two seconds later, he was picking it out of the hole.

At the 17th Hogan's drive appeared to be flying slightly right of the accepted line but he knew, as ever, what he was doing. It started to draw, and by the time it had run out of breath it was miles down the middle of the fairway. Faldo hit a good one too but he was fully 30 yards behind.

As Faldo walked after his ball he heard the cheers emanating from the 18th green. Moments later he saw Jacklin haring up the fairway and by the time Faldo had reached his ball he knew about Langer's fate and that he had to win his match if Europe were to win the Ryder Cup.

That thought stored, he forgot about it. The only thing he was concentrating on was the shot in hand. His caddie, Fanny Sunesson, got out her little book and flicked to the pages detailing the hole's considerable list of problems. She told him how far he had to go. Both player and caddie were in agreement that he would need to hit a 4 iron. Aim it just on the swale to the right of the Road Hole Bunker and let it drift away to the centre of the green. Faldo saw no point in dabbling with the bunker. Even in the situation in which he found himself he still thought a par was a good score on this hole.

So did Hogan. And whatever Faldo had done with his second shot he would have thought the same and attempted to play the same shot. Now that Faldo lay 30 ft away in 2 he was more convinced than ever that he was right. 'If you ever see me anywhere near that bunker you know that I have played a bad shot,' he had told a couple of American journalists the previous afternoon.

He played a bad shot. The ball's flight was directly over Faldo's line at its launch but again it had been hit with a touch of draw and now it was clear that Hogan was going to have a few anxious seconds as he watched to see if the ball finished in the Road Hole Bunker or not. It pitched just short of the green and ran over the corner of the swale. The ball was now under the influence of its contours. It swerved around towards the bunker. But it still had some momentum left and as it began to swing perilously close to the sand it freed itself and leapt above the slope. Now it was influenced by another contour and this one was edging it ever closer to the hole. When the ball came to a halt it was just 6 ft away. Of course, no one in the gallery knew that Hogan had been planning a stroke altogether less audacious. They just thought it was another miracle shot in a week when they had witnessed more than their fair share. The American players who had walked down the 18th fairway to witness this scene were now flinging their arms in the air and shouting their delight. But even after such a shot the outcome was not decided. It was no different in fact from that at the 14th. What if Faldo were to hole? Then Hogan would once more have to sink his putt not to be 1 down playing the 18th.

Faldo would hardly have been human if this thought hadn't crossed his mind, and the momentous circumstances caused him to take even longer over the putt. As he struck it Faldo instinctively thought it was in. He said so later and his body language indicated as much. He was ready to spin around and salute the crowd and salute his team-mates but it was the ball that did the spinning. It caught the left edge of the hole and spun out. Faldo was heartbroken. He slumped to his knees. When he looked up he saw his opponent coming towards him, holding his ball. Hogan placed it in Faldo's hands. He showed no emotion. He went back towards the hole and replaced his ball marker with his own ball. Hogan didn't take long to weigh up the putt. He didn't think about what it meant and how it would decide whether the Ryder Cup was won or whether the suspense was to continue for another hole. He just stepped right up to it and holed it. Hogan acknowledged the cheers from all those with American interests at heart. Those features that had appeared cast in stone suddenly broke out into a smile as he looked at his colleagues. Hagen was weeping gently and clapping and shouting hoarsely in Hogan's ear: 'You didn't really play that shot to go so close to the bunker, did you?' Hogan discouraged approaches from anyone else. He still hadn't won his match.

If Faldo could have won the 18th and so halved his game it would have meant a tie for the Ryder Cup. But he couldn't get the 3 required. It was as if what had happened at the 17th had squeezed some of the life out of him. In the end he made a 5 to lose his match by 2 holes. Hogan had finished 3, 3, 3, 4.

It was golf fit to give America the Ryder Cup by the closest possible margin at 14½ points to 13½. Jacklin congratulated Hagen and each of his players in turn, shaking all their hands. There appeared tears in his eyes too, but if he was disappointed at the outcome he was doing a good job at hiding it. He looked as if he was just honoured to have witnessed such a stupendous day's golf.

The players walked off towards the locker room. Twenty minutes later they returned wearing jackets, with the Americans wearing broad smiles as well. The scene that greeted them resembled the opening ceremony with chairs either side of the podium to rest their aching limbs. They saw former President George Bush present the trophy to the triumphant Hagen. They heard the two captains say how proud they were of all their efforts. They heard Jacklin say that the 17th, the most feared hole in the game, had been conquered this week by the two best shots that he had ever seen. They heard both say how the players' performance had enhanced the standing of the sport. And they heard the crowds, who had loyally stayed behind, cheer them all and clap and stamp their feet when they eventually made their weary way to the sanctuary of the R&A clubhouse.

And soon they were gone, back to the worlds from which they came. The lights in the media tent were still on but most journalists had now finished their work and were preparing to leave. In the clubhouse the members were enjoying one last drink.

The official dinner for the players had ended and most of the Americans were now on Concorde, travelling back to their own land with the coveted prize.

Hagen had not joined them. He was having a drink with O'Connor, Woosnam, Barnes and Jacklin in the Old Course Hotel. In the morning he would be on his way to Germany.

While Hagen stayed in Europe, his opposite number would be catching an afternoon flight the following day from Edinburgh to London and then on Tuesday he would be off back to his life on the US Senior tour. First there was a press conference in the morning, when he would break the news that this was the end of the road as far as his Ryder Cup captaincy was concerned. Jacklin looked shattered. In some ways it was a sad note on which to end but the golf had been sublime. Each of the last five singles matches had come to a finish on the home hole at the Home of Golf and it had come down to a putt here and a putt there. For a moment he thought about Ballesteros, and wondered what he was doing.

Ballesteros was in his room, and was looking back down the course towards the clubhouse. His mind looked blank. The clubhouse's floodlights were on and the 18th green was just visible. It was a lovely, though desolate, scene as a single spectator stood and stared and raised his collar against the gathering breeze.

Results

Day One
FOURSOMES

Barnes & Gallacher LOST to Hogan & Nicklaus 3 and 2
Faldo & Oosterhuis HALVED with Nelson & Watson
Woosnam & O'Connor LOST to Kite & Lema by 1 hole
Ballesteros & Olazabal BEAT Mangrum & Snead by 1 hole
EUROPE: 1½ USA: 2½

FOURBALLS

Brown & Lyle BEAT Palmer & Sarazen 4 and 2
Woosnam & O'Connor LOST to Nicklaus & Hogan 2 and 1
Cotton & Langer BEAT Trevino & Casper 2 and 1
Ballesteros & Olazabal HALVED with Mangrum & Snead
EUROPE: 4 USA: 4

Day Two
FOURSOMES

Cotton & Langer HALVED with Hogan & Nicklaus
Faldo & Oosterhuis BEAT Kite & Lema 4 and 3
Woosnam & O'Connor HALVED with Nelson & Watson
Ballesteros & Olazabal BEAT Snead & Mangrum by 1 hole
EUROPE: 7 USA: 5

FOURBALLS

Barnes & Gallacher BEAT Nelson & Nicklaus by 1 hole
Ballesteros & Olazabal LOST to Palmer & Trevino 3 and 2
Brown & Lyle LOST to Snead & Mangrum by 2 holes
Faldo & Cotton HALVED with Sarazen & Casper
EUROPE: 8½ USA: 7½

Day Three
SINGLES

Woosnam LOST to Nicklaus 3 and 2
Ballesteros BEAT Palmer by 1 hole
Olazabal HALVED with Snead
Brown BEAT Trevino by 1 hole
O'Connor LOST to Watson 2 and 1
Gallacher LOST to Kite 3 and 2
Lyle LOST to Lema 2 and 1
Oosterhuis HALVED with Mangrum
Barnes BEAT Casper by 1 hole
Cotton HALVED with Sarazen
Langer HALVED with Nelson
Faldo LOST to Hogan by 2 holes

EUROPE: 13½
USA: 14½